To ANTHONY

ABEL F. Ortega

COURAGE ON BATAAN AND BEYOND

Abel Sr. and Abel Jr. at Lake Marble Falls, Texas, 2003

Memories of an American POW who was a
slave of the Japanese during WWII for 3 ½ years

BY
ABEL ORTEGA JR.

FOREWORD BY
DUANE HEISINGER, CAPT., U.S. NAVY (RET.)

authorHOUSE™

1663 LIBERTY DRIVE, SUITE 200
BLOOMINGTON, INDIANA 47403
(800) 839-8640
WWW.AUTHORHOUSE.COM

First published by AuthorHouse 09/23/05

ISBN: 1-4208-6384-3 (sc)

Library of Congress Control Number: 2005905136

Printed in the United States of America
Bloomington, Indiana

This book is printed on acid-free paper.

This book is about my father,
my Hero, from your son
Abel Ortega Jr.

Abel Sr. and Abel Jr. in 1966

Abel Sr. and Abel Jr. at the finish of the 26.2 mile Marathon Run/March at the White Sands Missile Range Army Base in New Mexico, 2004, to honor the "Heroes of Bataan" and the sacrifices they made.

Battling Bastards of Bataan

"We're the Battling Bastards of Bataan,
No mamma, no papa, no Uncle Sam,
No aunts, no uncles, no cousins, no nieces,
No pills, no planes, no artillery pieces,
And nobody gives a damn!"

By Frank Hewlett, 1942

Abel F. Ortega

1945

Table of Contents

Foreword

The Japanese attacked the Philippines within hours of Pearl Harbor in December of 1941. America was not prepared in either place. About twenty-five thousand Americans had earlier been sent to assist in the anticipated need to defend this island nation located seven thousand miles west of California and about six hundred miles south of Japanese-controlled Formosa. Most of these men had been activated from National Guard forces and arrived only a few months or weeks before the war commenced. The odds were close to hopeless for the Filipino-American forces, for in most cases they had been given outdated equipment and ammunition stockpiled from WWI with which to fight. The Japanese military was modern and battle-tested from years of fighting in China and for the most part had quality equipment. No relief from the east was possible, and the Filipino-American forces soon came to realize that they were expendable. After four months of fighting on the Bataan Peninsula, and another month on Corregidor, the surrender of Corregidor Island became necessary. Unlike Hawaii, the war for these far-flung American and Philippine forces continued for months. Then, as prisoners of war, it continued for years. These men had given five valuable months of fighting for the necessary buildup of supplies in the United States. This military buildup and delaying action may have prevented a Japanese invasion of Australia.

As POWs, the odds of surviving for these men were low. But, no one had anticipated that starvation, disease, forced labor and barbaric treatment would be part of their treatment under the Japanese. Abel F. Ortega shares within his writing the months and years branded in his memory of his life as a prisoner. His personal faith, youth, strong family ties and a deep ingrained desire to return helped sustain him through the worst of the treatment and indignities of those years. The reader is brought along into his personal agony and will gain a clear understanding of Abel's thoughts during his time in the camps and on the Japanese Hell Ships.

It would be impossible otherwise for any of us who did not suffer the ravages of war as a Japanese prisoner in World War II to imagine or sense, with any accurate degree, what really took place during Bataan combat, then as a POW on the Death March and the years of imprisonment. But within *Courage on Bataan and Beyond*, written carefully, but with masterful sensitivity by Abel with the close assistance of his son, Abel, Jr., one can gain some understanding of those days. We are brought along and somehow, we can understand. We should all see and appreciate the special relationship of father and son, for in the writing it is the son, Abel Ortega, Jr., who wants to ensure that his father's story is not lost, but will be told for the generations of the Ortega family, researchers and historians yet to come who might not otherwise know the events of those days over sixty years ago. There is much here to know.

In the comfort in which most of us live our lives today, even the headiest of imaginations cannot bring us to fully understand the events of those WWII POW days. Who can comprehend the bestial handling of these men as they staggered along on the Bataan Death March, or the inhumane handling of the innocent Filipino civilians along the way north to that first POW area, Camp O'Donnell? Who of us can sense the deep hunger and thirst beyond description during those hot and humid tropical temperatures of April 1942, while these POWs were struggling along those primitive roads on the march north—and within the impossibly crowded conditions on the boxcars and within the darkened holds of the Hell Ships? The endemic malaria and dengue fever of the Philippines, along with deliberate food deprivation in the camps, created deadly conditions. Ultimately, over the years of imprisonment, these continued conditions, along with diseases and illnesses aggravated by lack of sustaining food, caused over five thousand deaths in just the early months of imprisonment. Over 38% of these men died during the years of POW time, but no help was given. Who of us but in seeing pictures of the weakened and dissipated men who did survive Bilibid Prison, Cabanatuan Camp and the Japanese POW Hell Ships can understand that few of these men could even recognize their friends who were lying next to them, still alive, but unrecognizable from their shrunken appearances and haggard faces.

It is important that we each know what took place during those days in the Philippines where our country placed unprepared men with ancient equipment on shores where they had no chance of being reinforced or relieved if war came—as it did. Inhumanity was common and compassion not often observed. In *Courage on Bataan and Beyond* you will know. Read well, know and understand.

Duane Heisinger,
January 2005,
Fairfax, Virginia,

Author of
Father Found,
Xulon Press, 2003

Duane Heisinger, the oldest of three sons of Grace and Lawrence Heisinger, was born in 1930 and raised in Fresno, California. After two years at Fresno State College and a year in the U.S. Air Force, Duane entered the U.S. Naval Academy, graduating an Ensign in 1956. He served 30 years in the Navy, retiring as a Navy Captain. His assignments were primarily at sea—including two ship commands and three combat tours in Vietnam—and over eleven years in overseas intelligence assignments—including three years as the Defense Attaché in London. In recent years he has been engaged in research covering the life and death of his father as a POW of the Japanese in the Philippines during WWII. Duane and his wife, Judith, live in Virginia. They have three married daughters and ten grandchildren.

Preface

The men and women of World War II fought and died for our freedom so that we may live in this wonderful country called America. They inspired us with their character, courage under pressure and determination to succeed. The sacrifices they made cannot be measured or matched. I am proud to say that my father fought bravely and heroically in two wars, World War II and Korea. He did it because he loved his country, his flag and the principles they stood for. He believed in duty, honor and country. I truly believe that he is part of the "Greatest Generation."

During World War II, in the Philippine Islands, he survived over five months of intense and fierce battle engagements with the Japanese Army, with little to no food, water, medical supplies or ammunition. The food on Bataan was almost non-existent. By mid-January, they were cut down to half-rations, and by mid-February, they were on less than 1,000 calories a day. That is not enough to keep soldiers healthy and their immune systems strong. The Japanese thought they would take the Philippines in a little over a month, but the soldiers of Bataan held out from December 8th, 1941, to April 9th, 1942. Their supply line was cut off because the ships were sunk at Pearl Harbor. The remaining supply ships were diverted to Europe by order of President Roosevelt, and Bataan was sacrificed. To make matters worse, the soldiers who fought on Bataan were plagued with tropical diseases, malaria and malnutrition, but they did not give up. They continued to fight with determination; courage and a will to survive that cannot be fully described. As General MacArthur was ordered to leave Bataan and head for Australia, he said, "I shall return," but the soldiers did not think it would be three years later. General MacArthur wanted them to fight to the last man and hold the Philippines. These men did not surrender! Lieutenant General Jonathan Wainwright went against General MacArthur's orders and surrendered them in order to save as many lives as possible due to the condition of the men. Approximately 78,000 American and Filipino soldiers surrendered to the Japanese. This was the first time in American history that an army this size had to surrender to an enemy force. These men had fought heroically for so long, and so many good soldiers' lives had been lost that the thought of surrendering was traumatic for them. This was an emotionally and psychologically hard decision for some of the men including my father. They were called the "Battling Bastards of Bataan" because they had been forgotten.

My father had never really talked about his experiences in great detail until recently. Some of the stories he has told have brought tears to his eyes. I know it was hard for him to remember some of those painful memories, but I feel that they needed to be *told so his friends and family can truly understand what he went through and know that war is awful, though necessary in some cases. I know the tears he has shed were not just from the memories of his days as a POW, but also for the dead soldiers and childhood friends he lost.*

There were so many POWs who were in different situations that each one has his or her own story about what they saw and what happened to them. Dad and I are going to try and tell you about his experiences and survival of the Bataan Death March, two Hell Ship voyages, and three and a half years as a prisoner of war. The book will be based on conversations, videotapes, and audiotapes he has made over the years. There will be some of my thoughts and feelings expressed throughout the book in italics because of how I feel towards my father and the men he fought with. I have done research at the National Archives in Baltimore, Maryland, read a countless number of books that have been written by fellow POWs, their sons, daughters, best-selling authors, and viewed web sites dedicated to the heroes of Bataan.

The Early Years of WWII

Pictures taken after basic training 1941

Pictures taken after basic training 1941

Pictures taken after basic training 1941

The Beginning

On August 22nd, 1919, I was born to Ruben and Deborah Ortega. I was the fifth child born into this family, but there was something unusual about my birth. Before I was born, my mother spent days and nights crying and she could not understand why. She had never cried like this with any of her other children. I'm sure that later in life, when I became a prisoner of the Japanese, she might have understood why. So my mother gave me more than her share of love so that I would become the fattest little baby of our family. Oh, I loved my mother very much and was always trying to do things around the house that would please her. My mother could always depend upon me when my other brothers didn't want to run the errands. I can hear my mother now "Abelito, por favor anda a la tienda por mi. Tus hermanos son unos flojotes que no puedo hacerles que vayan a la tienda por mi. Tu papa viene a comer muy pronto y no tengo nada que prepararle." Translated in English, "Abel, please, come and run this errand for me to the store. Your brothers are a bunch of ol' lazy bones, and I can't even get them to go to the store for me. Your daddy's coming home for lunch pretty soon, and I haven't a thing ready for him."

As I got older, it was my custom to rock in the rocking chair in the living room, because I loved to just sit and rock. One time when I was about thirteen years of age, I was in the rocking chair in the living room rocking away, when in walks my father. He looks to mom and said "Mother, here is your Abelito, your piensa lo mucho," which in English means "the thinker." Everybody in the family called me "piensa lo mucho." That's exactly what I was doing. While I was in school studying geography, I developed a great desire to learn about and visit the Orient. I thought about Japan, China, India, and all of the thousands of islands across the Pacific Ocean and wondered what life would be like. I would sit in the rocking chair and think to myself that it sure would be nice to go and visit the Orient. Since my family was not a rich family, I would become sad at the thought that I would probably never get a chance to visit.

When I became a young man, I participated in all the sports, such as baseball, softball, and swimming. I always loved keeping myself in top physical shape. Little did I know how important it would be to be in top condition, mentally and physically, and little did I know how that I would need all my strengths in the years that were ahead of me.

I was twenty-one years old when Germany was marching across Europe and Japan's negotiations were uncertain. I received my draft notice to join the army in March of 1941, and was required to report to Fort Sam Houston for processing. There was only one problem: I was under the minimum weight requirement for enlisting. I found myself having to eat two dozen bananas so I could make the weight before I had to report for processing. I made the weight and stayed at Fort Sam Houston for a few weeks before being sent to Fort Knox, Kentucky, for training in the art of warfare. I was the first of six Ortega boys to have to report for duty in WWII. Yes, there were six Ortega boy's in WWII at the same time. Eliseo and I were in the Pacific, Ruben was in Alaska, and Sam, Ben and Daniel were in Europe. Daniel paid the ultimate sacrifice on the beaches of Normandy.

Dad as a baby in 1919

Daniel, Ben, Abel

The Ortega's

Sam, Daniel, Abel, Ben, Ruben, Eliseo, Deborah and Martha

Basic Training
Fort Knox, Kentucky

I was sent by train to Fort Knox, Kentucky, from Fort Sam Houston in April of 1941 for basic training. We stayed in brand new barracks that had just been built. They were a luxury compared to the tents at Fort Sam Houston. The food was another story, though. When we first arrived, it was great, but after a few days it went downhill. Everyone was complaining about the quality and quantity of food we were getting. After enough complaints, there was an investigation by the lieutenant as to why the food was bad. We later found out the first sergeant in charge of the mess hall was stealing a lot of the food and selling it on the outside. I don't know whatever happened to him afterward, but the food did get better.

My unit in basic training was AFRTC 8th Battalion, Company B. I was really gung ho when I got there. I wanted to be the best soldier Uncle Sam had to offer. I wanted to be the best shot, the best marcher, and to outdo everyone on the conditioning and physical tests. Since I was in such good shape physically, basic wasn't that hard for me, and all those things came easily. In fact, I was always the best in all of the agility and conditioning skills. There was one sad moment in basic training for me. The older of my two sisters died while giving birth back home in Austin, so I had leave for a few days. Her name was Deborah.

8th Battalion Co. B Fort Knox, Kentucky, May 17th, 1941

753rd G.H.Q. Tank Battalion
Camp Polk, Louisiana

After I finished basic training at Fort Knox, I was sent to Camp Polk, Louisiana, for formal training as a radio operator. I was assigned to the 753rd G.H.Q. Tank Battalion, Med. Tanks Company A. They had just built a brand new area of the camp and that's where we were. Because of the draft and the overwhelming amount of soldiers, almost all of the bases in the United States and Hawaii were building new barracks for the soldiers. It was nice to have new barracks again. I pretty much kept to myself during basic training as well as at this camp. There weren't very many Mexicans there, and since I didn't drink, curse, play cards, or chase women, I didn't fit in very well with the other soldiers. We all got along, but I didn't have any good buddies I would run around with. On the weekends I would go into town and walk around, see a picture show, or hit the soda fountain and have an ice-cold ceda (soda) for those non-Ortega's. Other times, I would just stay at camp and read a book and rest.

I was sent to radio operator's school, maybe because I spoke both Spanish and English. All I know is that I did not want to learn that skill, but that's where they sent me anyway. I would sit and stare out the windows where we learned to do our dots and dashes and would watch all the armored vehicles— tanks, jeeps, and half-tracks—and wish I were with them. I thought to myself that if I were to fail the tests they gave me, then maybe I would be transferred to the armored unit. I took the final test and failed it on purpose. A few days later I was transferred to the tanks, and I was so happy that I couldn't wait. In the meantime, the 192nd Tank Battalion, which consisted of Companies A, B, C, and D, were on maneuvers at the same time we were there.

753rd G.H.Q. Tank BN. Co. A Camp Polk, Louisiana, September 20th, 1941

192nd Tank Battalion
Camp Polk, Louisiana

In 1940, the 32nd Division National Guard Tank Company of Janesville, Wisconsin, reported for duty as the 192nd Tank Battalion Co. A. The 192nd was made up of four companies. Company A came from Janesville, Wisconsin; Company B from Maywood, Illinois; Company C from Port Clinton, Ohio; and Company D from Harrodsburg, Kentucky. On November 25, 1940, they traveled to Fort Knox, Kentucky, where they came together to form the 192nd GHQ Light Tank Battalion. In January 1941, they took men from the four letter companies of the battalion and formed Headquarters Company. After this was done, the army tried to fill the vacancies in the letter companies with men from the home states of each of the companies. After taking part in the Louisiana maneuvers in the late summer of 1941, on the side of a hill at Camp Polk, they learned that they were being sent overseas. Those soldiers who were at least 29 years of age were given the opportunity to resign their service so that left quite a few openings. The replacements they sought were from the 753rd Tank Battalion, the unit I was in.

When they had called our Battalion up for a meeting, the Commander asked if there were any volunteers who wanted to join the 192nd Tank Battalion and go to the Philippines. He said they needed replacements for men who had been discharged. With my love for the Orient, I was the first to step forward. If I had known what was to lie ahead, I never would have volunteered. All of the volunteers were placed in different companies, and I ended up in Company A. I did not know any of the men in that Battalion because I had been with the 753rd during the maneuvers. All of the men in Company A were from Janesville and had been together for a long time. They were all best friends, brothers and had been well-trained in their local National Guard unit.

After our first meeting, I was assigned to the half-track section of our company and introduced to Capt. Walter H. Write, the Commander of Company A. He asked me if I had ever driven a half-track before, and I said, "No." He took me over to a half-track and asked me to drive with one of the other guys. We went for a ride and since I was a quick learner, I got the hang of it very quickly.

I was given a half-track that had a roller in the front for going up hills, through ditches and ravines. On the top above me was a .50 caliber machine gun mounted on a swivel turret. That gun would really do some damage to whatever it hit. I was also trained on and was given a Tommy Machine Gun to go with my .45 caliber pistol.

The Trip to the Philippines

Soon after I joined the 192nd, we were given our secret orders to go to the Philippines. Our code name was PLUM. It was supposed to be a secret, but everyone found out about it, even the locals. I guess that goes to show you how good our secret orders were kept secret. All of our tanks and half-tracks had to be loaded on the flatbed train cars. That took a while, since the tanks and half-tracks were new to us; some of the guys were not too good at driving them yet. We headed out of Camp Polk, Louisiana, by train to Angel Island by San Francisco around October 20, 1941. During the trip, we made a stop in New Mexico. We had to make several stops and check all the cables and straps due to the heavy load of tanks and half-tracks. Back in those days, people lived really close to the train tracks so I saw a lady outside hanging her laundry on the line. She lived about seventy-five yards away from where we were. I yelled at her, "Do you have any tortillas?" She replied, "Yes, come and get some." I jumped off the train and ate a few of them while we talked. After I ate the tortillas, I took some back to the guys on the train. Since they were from Wisconsin, they asked,

"What are those?" I said, "They are tortillas, man, eat 'em." A few of the guys called them "Mexican Pies," and they all loved them. One of my jobs on the train was guard duty. I was given a .45 caliber pistol and was told to make sure all the lights were out and that nobody was up walking around at night.

We arrived at Angel Island on October 26th, 1941, and had all of our equipment off-loaded by local guys and loaded onto our ship. When I arrived at Angel Island, I stared across the Pacific and my mind carried me to the distant land that I was about to see. I thought about Japan, China and the women with their small feet and the men with their pigtails. I thought of the palm trees, the rice paddies, the temples, and all that I had learned in Geography. While we were at Angel Island, I was assigned to work on the small ship that ferried the guys back and forth from San Francisco. When the boats would come to the respective docks, I would jump off and tie the rope so the ship wouldn't slip away. I did that for a couple of days, and then had to pull KP on Angel Island for a day. We boarded the U.S.S. AP 43 Hugh L. Scott a few days later and sailed for Hawaii and Guam to drop off supplies, and then to the Philippines. We had a few days of great R&R in Hawaii. On our trip to the Philippines we had to zigzag across the ocean to keep from being tracked by the Japanese. One night while I was out on deck, I could see a ship, off in the distance, flashing its signal lights. One of the ships in our convoy went to check it out, but I never heard anything.

National Archives

USS AP43 Hugh L. Scott

Clark Field & the Philippines

We arrived in the Philippines on Thanksgiving Day, November 20, 1941. We were then sent to our designated briefing areas where we were to get our orders. They told us that this was top secret. We were there to help train the Filipino Army in tank warfare and operations, and later go on to China to help train their Nationalist Army.

Our tank battalion was sent by train to Fort Stotsenberg from Manila, which was next to Clark Field. We were housed in tents that had a wooden floor and a couple of windows. Since there were so many soldiers showing up, they ran out of barracks and made us use tents. I hadn't eaten all day, so I looked up a friend of mine named Joel Ruiz, from Austin, Texas, who was with the 200th CA and had been stationed there at Fort Stotsenberg. I found him and asked if there was anything to eat. He went into the kitchen and found some bread and gravy, and that's what I had for my Thanksgiving Day meal: a gravy sandwich. Since we were ignorant of the Philippine language, most everyone thought it was Spanish, and so the guys in my unit were trying all of a sudden to be my buddy, thinking I could get some local women for them. We came to find out later that their language is Tagalog, so my buddies pretty much left me alone again, and I lost all my friends that I had made.

At that time, life was great in the Philippines. Each tent was assigned a houseboy. He would shine shoes, make beds and clean up after us. I thought to myself, this is great. In the meantime, the life of soldiering began, and we had to wash off all of our equipment after we arrived at camp. The salt water would do a number on the equipment if we didn't clean it. All of our guns were packed in cozmoline and had to be cleaned as well. We put the equipment in fifty gallon drums of boiling water so the grease would melt off. They were then reassembled, oiled and checked. We also had to load the ammo belts for our different guns one bullet at a time since there were no automatic loaders.

On December 8th in the Philippines (December 7th in the States), a little before lunch, we were in the lunch line with our mess kits when we were issued another warning of attack. We had already been under alert that morning, but that had been called off. This time, we immediately received orders to go and camouflage our equipment under the banana trees and tall grasses that were prevalent there. After we did that, you should have heard all the noise of the mess kits as everyone ran to back across the field to try and be first in line at the mess tent. They left Private William Curtis and me to guard the equipment since we were new to the outfit and had to do all the dirty work. He was sitting in his half-track, and I was sitting in mine, when all of a sudden, we heard a humming noise that got louder and louder. Lo and behold, we looked up and saw one of the most beautiful sights I have ever seen. It was a large formation of planes off in the distance. We counted fifty-six bombers coming over our heads, and I said, "William, isn't that a beautiful sight?" I then said, "Just think, when there is an emergency, the United States Army Air Corps is always there, ready to defend whatever needs defending." I had no sooner said those words, when all of a sudden we heard loud whistling noises all around us. The bombs were falling, and they were Japanese bombs. First the bombers came in and really let us have it. They took out almost all of the planes that were on the runway, buildings, barracks, fuel dumps, and even our mess tent. Then the fighters came in low and were strafing everything in sight that the bombers had missed.

Most everyone was at lunch when the bombs fell. It was horrible. The ground was shaking tremendously. There was smoke, shrapnel and debris flying all over the place. Our half-tracks were jumping off the ground about a foot or so from the impact of the bombs which were blowing up stuff all around us. My WWI helmet was banging against the dash, which didn't feel too good. Fires were blazing from the barracks, and people were screaming. There were people running for cover, and those who could get guns were firing and trying to do what they could. Some of the guys made it to their tanks and had a chance to try out the new 37 millimeter guns. The guys from the 200th CA were trying to fire some rounds, but I found out some didn't explode because they were from WWI and contained quite a few duds. A lot of our weapons and ammunition were from WWI and that would later pose a problem during close jungle combat situations with the tankers.

In the meantime, when the bombs started to fall, William and I jumped in our half-tracks, manned our .50-caliber machine guns, and cocked the levers back and unloaded on those Japanese planes with all we had. The first couple of times you fire at a moving target, you're a little off until you learn how much to lead the planes and watch your tracer bullets. I got really good at it in a hurry, but with all the smoke and fires around us, I don't know if I took any of them out. I would like to think that I put a few holes in those red-circle planes. I know one thing though: I had that machine gun so hot it was smoking. I even threw a few rounds at them with my Tommy gun. Between William and me, we put a lot of lead in the air. I had been practicing being a soldier, and now at the age of twenty-two, I was one. I obtained more ammunition and manned my .50 caliber machine gun again.

Since we weren't prepared for the attack, there were no foxholes dug, so the guys jumped into whatever hole they could find. Finally the all-clear was given, and we went back to our tents to assess the damage that had been done. Most of the planes that had been on the runways at Clark Field were destroyed, as well as most of the buildings at Fort Stotsenberg. The bombings continued for a few more weeks. There was some humor in the lull of bombings. By this time, we had a chance to dig our foxholes, but on one occasion the bombers caught us off guard. The Captain jumped into the first ditch he saw but should've looked first. After the bombing run was over and when he stood up, everyone saw him but was too afraid to say anything. After a few seconds, the First Sergeant started laughing, and then we knew it was okay to laugh with him. The ditch the Captain had jumped into was the latrine. The humor didn't last long because the reality of war was here.

Our tank units were ordered deep into the jungles and on the coastlines to head off the Japanese landings at Lingayen Gulf. My half-track, along with some others, was ordered to stay behind and guard the base from Japanese paratroopers who were rumored to be arriving soon. That did not happen, so some of the guys left to support the tanks of our battalion. Throughout the month of December, the Japanese were landing on different areas of Luzon, the main island we were on. Captain Write told me to stay behind with Sergeant Dale Lawton and my radioman, Private Joseph Mcrea. We were to try and procure some food and supplies since everyone had left in such a hurry. We got what supplies we could from the base commissary and PX since it had been abandoned by the locals who had helped run it. We headed up to the North Luzon Force Headquarters at Bamban to meet up with the guys in our battalion.

By the time we arrived, we were already fighting a retreating battle from Lingayen Gulf down to Mariveles, which is in the Bataan Peninsula of Luzon. It was a tough battle. The Japanese had outmanned us and had better equipment. Our tank design flaws would become prevalent during the first tanks battles of WWII. We had small 37 millimeter guns and straight sides with thin riveted metal. When one of our tanks would get hit, the rivets would explode inside the tanks causing severe injury and, in some cases, death to the crew. On the other hand, the Japanese tanks had larger caliber guns and sloping sides that caused our 37 millimeter shells to bounce off.

One time, during a battle engagement, I had pulled up to the front lines where all the action was with the tanks. Since I was the communication half-track, I had to be close to the action, but this time my radio operator and I parked and walked up to where the action was. There was a guy by the name of Miles Weech from Idaho who I got along with pretty well and was one of the tankers. He and I would always draw our .45s against each other as if we were in the Old West. I guess it was because I was from Texas and he was from Idaho, and it was a cowboy thing. I never could beat him at the draw because he was so fast. He was a funny guy who made me laugh a lot. He was about fifty yards in front of me when his tank was hit. He and his crewman jumped out of the tank and started running towards me when he was shot in the stomach. His crewman saw me there with my submachine gun and ran over to me. He was in such a rage that he grabbed it from me and started running in the direction of the Japanese firing it as he ran, concentrating on a particular palm tree. I guess he thought there was a sniper in there. When your buddies get killed right in front of you, it is a hard thing to see and handle. Miles Weech was taken to the hospital where he later died on February 5th, 1942.

Sometimes your emotions can get the best of you, like when my Captain was killed. Since I was his driver, we had become good friends. It was on

December 24th, 1941. As the infantry would retreat back, it was up to us tankers and half-tracks to try and hold the enemy back. It was very chaotic up on the front lines. Along with the troops moving back, the locals were also clogging up the roads with their carts, ponies, and water buffalo as they retreated. Captain Write, along with some Filipinos, had jumped in a jeep and headed back north to lay some mines to try and stop the advancing Japanese. These were crude mines made of dynamite with a flashlight fuse that were very sensitive to pressure. One of the mines exploded in his hands, causing severe injury. He remained alive for a few hours, still giving commands to the tank crews and trucks. Captain Write was a very special man, and I think the Lord had put me in his command. He liked me a lot because I was different than the rest of the guys in Company A. When we first met, he asked me about chili. He wanted to know how it tasted since he was from Wisconsin and didn't have chili up there. Since I was Hispanic, he thought I liked chili and ate it all the time, but actually I didn't like it, so I couldn't tell him much. For the short time I knew him, he was a great leader and a great friend. A few days later, Lieutenant Bloomfield was made acting commander of Company A.

Capt. Walter H. Write
Proviso East Research Project

As we made our retreat back into the peninsula of Bataan, I was given the assignment of patrolling a section of coastline to warn Headquarters of any landings by the Japanese. I would patrol up and down the coastline looking for the Japanese, in case they were making a beach landing. I would patrol with Lieutenant Henry M. Knox. On several occasions I was spotted by enemy aircraft but was able to drive into the trees and camouflage myself. During our retreat back, I met up with the mechanics of my company. They had taken a .50-caliber machine gun from a damaged airplane and made a tripod for it. Whenever we would camp, they would set it out in case we needed it. One time some Japanese planes flew over and dropped a few bombs. This was the first time we had a chance to use it. When the bombs fell, the guys ran for cover. I said, "Get on the gun man!" No one did, so I ran over to it, cocked the lever back and let the lead fly. By this time in the war I was not afraid anymore, and did what I could to try and make a difference. Those mechanics did a good job of building that gun, and it worked well.

I remember a time when we had camped, I decided to take a walk down to the edge of the beach for a quiet moment and take a break from death and destruction. I walked down to the edge of the beach with my .45, just in case I needed a little protection. I saw a lot of different colored fish in all different sizes and shapes doing their own thing, oblivious to what was going on around them. It was a beautiful sight. The water was so clear, and I could see everything. That brought a lot of happiness to me in spite of the war going on around me. On my way back to camp, I had to cross a clear stream with running water that emptied into the ocean, so I decided to take a swim and relax. I stripped off all my clothes and lay in the water with my head sticking out. I listened to all the birds, the water flowing past my head, and all the peaceful sounds of the jungle, even though in the distance I could hear the booming of artillery shells firing every now and then. For the most part, it was so peaceful I didn't want to leave. Just as I finished dressing, I heard some leaves crackling as if someone was walking. I knelt down and peered through the bushes to see what was making that noise. I saw a native pigmy walking with his spear. Behind him was his wife, and strapped to her back was a little baby. That was such a beautiful sight to see. I had studied them in geography, and I finally got a chance to see them as they are very reclusive.

This lull in fighting we had was such a welcome break. You see, the Japanese had thought they could take the Philippines in just a short time. They had been taught that the Americans were weak. Well, they had to use the lull to re-supply their troops from Singapore and other areas because we had ruined their plans to take the Philippines. What was supposed to be a one-month battle turned out to be a five-month battle from December 8th, 1941, to April 9th, 1942. Not to take anything away from Pearl Harbor, but they were bombed in one day. We were bombed for five months! General MacArthur sent a message telling us that help and supplies were on the way, but that never happened. It got our morale up a little, but deep down inside I knew it wasn't going to happen. By the time March 1942 came around we were already on 1,000-calories-a-day meals. That is not enough to sustain a fighting soldier, especially those that are suffering from tropical diseases and malnutrition.

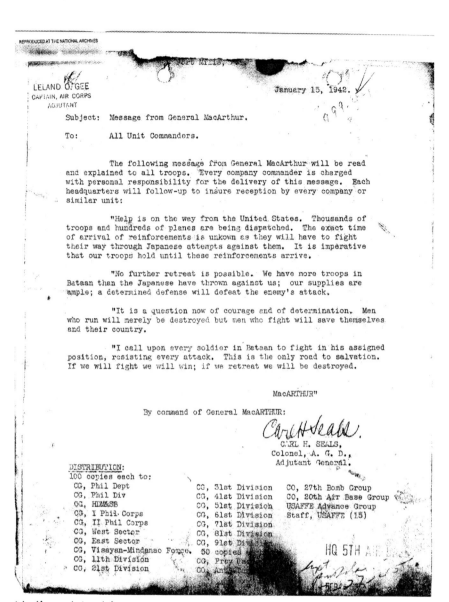

LELAND O. GEE
CAPTAIN, AIR CORPS
ADJUTANT

January 15, 1942.

Subject: Message from General MacArthur.

To: All Unit Commanders.

The following message from General MacArthur will be read and explained to all troops. Every company commander is charged with personal responsibility for the delivery of this message. Each headquarters will follow-up to insure reception by every company or similar unit:

"Help is on the way from the United States. Thousands of troops and hundreds of planes are being dispatched. The exact time of arrival of reinforcements is unkown as they will have to fight their way through Japanese attempts against them. It is imperative that our troops hold until these reinforcements arrive.

"No further retreat is possible. We have more troops in Bataan than the Japanese have thrown against us; our supplies are ample; a determined defense will defeat the enemy's attack.

"It is a question now of courage and of determination. Men who run will merely be destroyed but men who fight will save themselves and their country.

"I call upon every soldier in Bataan to fight in his assigned position, resisting every attack. This is the only road to salvation. If we will fight we will win; if we retreat we will be destroyed.

MacARTHUR"

By command of General MacARTHUR:

CARL H. SEALS,
Colonel, A. G. D.,
Adjutant General.

DISTRIBUTION:
100 copies each to:
CG, Phil Dept   CG, 31st Division   CO, 27th Bomb Group
CG, Phil Div   CG, 41st Division   CO, 20th Air Base Group
CG, HDM&SB   CG, 51st Division   USAFFE Advance Group
CG, I Phil Corps   CG, 61st Division   Staff, USAFFE (15)
CG, II Phil Corps   CG, 71st Division
CG, West Sector   CG, 81st Division
CG, East Sector   CG, 91st Division
CG, Visayan-Mindanao Force. 50 copies
CG, 11th Division   CG, Prov
CG, 21st Division   CO, An

HQ 5TH AIR

National Archives

Some of the diseases prevalent at this time were malaria, dengue fever, and diarrhea. All of our supply lines were cut off, and we had no way of getting food, medicine, and ammunition to continue the fight. It had gotten to the point that we didn't want to shoot anything to eat because we needed that extra ammunition. We had eaten all the Cavalry mules and horses, all the native caribou, and whatever else moved in the jungle. There were plenty of pythons to eat, along with lizards and monkeys. One time, one of the guys saw a monkey in the tree and we decided to eat it. He shot the monkey and skinned it, but afterwards, he held it up and it looked just like a little human baby, so he just threw it away. Another thing we learned was whatever the natives would eat; we would do the same too. When you are starving, you learn to adapt and overcome thoughts of what you are about to eat.

We were getting ready to make our last stand on Bataan when in March 1942 General Douglas MacArthur was ordered by President Roosevelt to leave for Australia. He sent a message for all those on Bataan to fight to the last man and gave command over to Lieutenant General Jonathan Wainwright. That was such a hard blow to us considering he had been on the island fortress of Corregidor, safe from all the bombings and supplied with food and medicine that we could have used.

HEADQUARTERS
United States Forces in the Philippines
Fort Mills, P. I.

March 23, 1942.

Subject: Message from General MacArthur.

To: All Units.

The following radiogram received March 21, 1942, from General MacArthur is published for the information of this Command:

"The President of the United States ordered me to break through the Japanese lines and proceed from Corregidor to Australia for the purpose, as I understand it, of organizing the American offensive against Japan, a primary objective of which is the relief of the Philippines. I came through and I shall return.

MacARTHUR."

By command of Lieutenant General WAINWRIGHT:

CARL H. SEALS,
Brigadier General, USA,
Adjutant General.

1b

National Archives

As we got close to the end of March, the fighting intensified. We fought with whatever we could throw at them. By this time the diseases were really taking a toll on the Allied forces there, and men were dying right and left. It was awful to see, because if we'd had enough medicine and food, most of the guys could have survived. Lieutenant General Jonathan Wainwright could see the toll this last stand was taking on the guys so he made the decision to surrender us. It was plain to see that some of the guys had lost their will to fight. He did this with the hope that we would survive and be treated according to the laws of the Geneva Convention. We came to find out Japan didn't sign the Geneva Convention and had no regard for humanity. We soon found out the true meaning of brutality. The Japanese did not care whether we lived or died.

The Surrender

I believe it was April 8th that our Captain called us to formation. He said, "I have just received word from our commanding General that we are ordered to surrender to the Japanese Imperial Forces. Men, as you know, we have run out of food, ammunition, medical supplies and all the necessary equipment to carry on this fight. I want all you men to go and destroy and get rid of all your equipment so that it will not fall into enemy hands and be used against us." I was very shocked and it was an extremely sad moment for me.

Many times in my youth, we had practically won every game in the sport of baseball. What made me sad was when we lost that last game for the city championship. In that moment of surrender, I had felt like I had lost that game all over again, but only worse. I was really sad and hurt. After all the hardship, deaths and heroic battles we had fought, it was very hard to surrender. I slowly made my way to my half-track, which I personally destroyed with a sledgehammer. I smashed the dashboard, the engine, the gun and the rear tracks. After I did that, I fell to ground on my knees and cried and cried just like a baby. After I had finished crying, I looked up to the sky through the trees and said these words, "Oh God, I don't want to die; I'm too young to die, but if it's your will Lord, I'm ready. But please Lord, please don't let me die. If you let me live, I'll do all I can to help my fellow prisoners in whatever may lay ahead." After I had finished talking with God, I cried some more. Just think, I was twenty-two years old and 8,000 miles away from home.

After lying there on the ground for some time, I dried the tears with the sleeves of my shirt and stood up, determined to face whatever may lie ahead. One of the thoughts that ran through my mind was to run into the jungles and hide and not permit myself to be captured. I started to do that but I had to come back because I remembered the promise I had made to God. At last I would get to see the enemy, the Japanese. They looked as bad as we did, with dirty uniforms, long mustaches, and scraggly beards. We marched to a town called Mariveles, which is on the Bataan peninsula. That is where we were to assemble for the Japanese. While we were at Mariveles, we could hear the artillery shells of the Japanese bombing Corregidor, which had not yet surrendered. Corregidor was the island fortress just off the tip of the Bataan Peninsula. That was where the high command was located at. The Japanese and Americans were battling it out. In the area where we were, it was raining confusion. No one knew what to do or where to go. There was no food or water and we were not permitted to try and locate these necessities. We couldn't depend on our officers because they didn't know anymore than we did. It was a long day; the hours were long, the minutes were long, and yes, even the seconds were long. I did not like this situation at all. I had heard that we were moving north, so I located a group of guys from my company. There was only one road north so we proceeded on foot. After we had gone a couple of hundred yards, we encountered an artillery shell battle between the Japanese and Corregidor. We certainly didn't expect this situation on our march; but what were we to expect being prisoners of war for the first time? One of the shells from Corregidor hit a Japanese artillery placement right in front of us. They were blown sky high and sent us scattering for cover. We were totally at their mercy with no cover and no way to protect ourselves.

The road we were on led right in front of the Japanese artillery placements, which put us right in the middle of the battle. One of the guys from our company was a mechanic, and he ran back to Mariveles to get a two-and-a-half-ton truck we had driven there but were ordered to abandon by the Japanese. After he hot-wired the truck, he came back and picked us up. We drove that old truck as fast as we could, dodging artillery shells and the craters they were making in the road. It was a bad situation, and all we could do was pray that we would make it. The guys who didn't have a truck had to run the whole distance, which I would guess to be a couple of miles. We finally made it through and the Japanese made us get off the truck and then confiscated it. One of our officers didn't make it to the end. Lieutenant Bloomfield died at the end just as we made it. He was not on a truck, so he had to run the whole distance, causing him to die of exhaustion. There was no place to bury him so we did the best we could on the side of the road to give him a decent burial. This was just the beginning of what was to become the march of death.

The Bataan Death March

Oh the march, what can I say about the March? There are no words to describe the humiliation, death, beatings, starvation and total lack of regard for human life we were faced with on this seven-day march of death. We walked sixty-five miles to San Fernando and rode a "Hell Train" boxcar for twenty-four miles to Capas. We then had to march another seven miles to Camp O'Donnell. In the minds of the Japanese, if you surrendered, you were not worthy to live. We were lower than dogs to them, so that's how we were treated. It's been estimated that approximately 78,000 Americans, Filipinos, and civilians started this march with about 60,000 to 65,000 surviving and reaching the first camp. The Japanese had underestimated the enormous amount of people and were not prepared for this. We were starved, sick and had been fed on less than 1,000 calories a day rations. We were not capable of making this march and it was evident by the number of dead that were on the sides of the road and in the ditches. Some were bayoneted, decapitated, shot, and run over by the Japanese trucks.

Proviso East Research Project

Bataan Death March

BATAAN PENINSULA
and
Route of the Death March

SFPS.k12.NM.US/Academy/Bataan/Intro.HTML

43

As soon as we were ordered off the truck, we were grouped up and made to kneel at a makeshift assembly area. The Japanese officer in charge made a speech, first in Japanese then in broken English, and expected us to understand. He instructed us to put all of our personal belongings out in front of us so they could take them. Some of the officers would not give up their rings, so the guards would chop off the finger and take the ring. They took watches and whatever else they thought they could use. Some of the guards looked into your mouth to see if you had gold fillings. There were a couple of guys who had their teeth knocked out because of that. As a Christian boy growing up, this was very hard to deal with. The situation was very chaotic because the guards were yelling at us in Japanese because some of the guys were taking their time. We were hot, thirsty, hungry and sick. We did not know what they were saying but we learned quickly by the point of a bayonet. At this location, they were separating the civilians from the soldiers. In the distance you could hear the cries of the mothers as their sons were taken away because the Japanese thought they were part of the war.

National Archives

Bataan Death March

Before I put my bag down in front of me, I dug a small hole and put my compass in it and covered it up. I then put my bag on top of it and hoped they would not find it. I had thought to myself that if I was ever in a situation where I had to get away into the jungle, I wanted my compass so I could find my way around. Well, they didn't find it and I was able to put it back into my pocket as we stood up to start the march. As we started on our march, the noise of war got fainter and fainter. In a way, I was glad to get away from the noise of war, but little did I know it would last for three and a half years.

We saw some ghastly scenes as we first started this march and they got worse as it went on. There were burned-out trucks, buses, and military trucks littered all over the place. There were dead Filipino soldiers bloated up, with flies swarming around them. The smell was unbearable and is something I'll never forget.

Due to the enormous amount of prisoners, we were put into groups of about forty. There were about ten rows with four in each row. I managed always to stay in the middle because I felt that was the safest place to be. As we would march, the Japanese guards who were on horseback would ride by and whack the guys on the outside with their swords as they rode by. By the first mile or so it was more of a mass group than an organized march.

National Archives

Bataan Death March

I was not used to brutality and terror; I had never seen this before. I had never seen soldiers treated like this and it really struck me deep down inside especially for a boy who never missed a day of Sunday school. On this march it was really hard for us to understand what they wanted us to do. We wanted to learn their language, but under these circumstances it was hard. There were many a skull cracked by the butt of the Japanese rifle if you didn't do what they wanted. Some of the guys would just stand there and try to figure out what they wanted us to do. Some of those guys got bayoneted or hit by rifle butts, sticks, or whatever the Japanese had closest to them at that time. I thought to myself, I am going to have to get used to this brutality or die trying to fight it.

When I started, I hadn't eaten in about two days and the water in my canteen was getting old. I learned very quickly how to manage my water intake. This was the hottest part of the year in the Philippines and the heat was unbearable. The road we were marching on was a mix of caliche and chunks of asphalt that had been torn up by tanks, trucks, and the bombs that hit it. It was really difficult to keep in step, or even walk, especially when the dust that was kicked up choked you. I witnessed some of the worst brutality imaginable on this march. Some of the guys hadn't eaten or had anything to drink in days. There were quite a few of them who didn't even have shoes. Their eyes were sunken in their heads and faces were covered in sweat. The Japanese kept prodding these guys on with the tips of their bayonets. A lot of them just gave up. They had no desire to live anymore and didn't care what happened to them. Once you gave up you were dead. I didn't want to give up. I had a strong will to survive and my faith in God kept me alive. I was not about to let the Japanese get the best of me.

National Archives

Bataan Death March

We had come to our first stop in the road when I noticed that some of the prisoners were looking at me and yelling and cursing obscenities for no reason at all. They were blaming me for their agony and the predicament that they were in. They had thought that I was a Filipino and they were really getting hostile towards me. I really felt sad and deeply hurt that my fellow soldiers were treating me this way. I tried to defend myself by telling them that I was an American from Texas, but with all their hollering and shouts, they didn't hear a word I said. Not only did I have to deal with hostile Japanese guards, but I was also faced with having to deal with hostile American prisoners taking this situation out on me.

I will never forget Eugene Greenfield from Minerva, Ohio. We took training together at Camp Polk, Louisiana. I had tried to take part in all the athletic events we had there at Camp Polk, but I always noticed Eugene sitting and watching instead of playing. In my mind I would always say to myself, "Look at that old lazy bone." Things change, and they certainly did on that road in Bataan. Eugene became one of my best friends and we helped each other on the march. When the soldiers had become hostile towards me, Eugene jumped to his feet and gave a wonderful speech on my behalf. He told them that I was an American and that my forefathers were in America before the white man came. It was a fine speech and is something I will never forget. He may not have been a participant in sports, but he was gifted in the use of words. He stood up for me that day and is what I would call a true American.

We continued on the march, leaving the combat areas and getting closer to the rear echelon of the Japanese lines. The brutality would get worse as the march continued on. I could see prisoners in front of me for miles and the same far behind me. We started to see the dead bodies of American soldiers on the side of the road that had become victims of the Japanese bayonets and swords. Their bodies were swollen and covered with blow flies. They had been stabbed for falling out of line and had been unable to get up. Some of the prisoners were even decapitated along with being bayoneted. On the sides of the road were algae-covered caribou wallows, full of flies. The prisoners who had not had any water for days couldn't hold back. They ran to the water and drank what they could before they were shot or bayoneted. Those that made it back to the line didn't last long. They would eventually become victims of dysentery and malaria. Those prisoners could not keep up on the march. The Japanese guards made the other prisoners beat them until they got up. If they didn't, they were killed. This was just the beginning of the march, and I had wondered how long I could take this brutality. We had no idea where we were going or how long we would be marching. Sometimes we would march until dark and you couldn't see where you were going. I remember seeing and hearing the cries of the prisoners but there was nothing I could do. There were times when you were walking and all you would see was a smashed bloody uniform in the tracks of a tank or truck. The Japanese would not drive around the dead or the ones that had fallen and were laying there still alive. They would just drive right over them again and again, smashing them into the ground until there was nothing left to recognize as a human. I wondered if the brutality would get worse for the thousands and thousands of prisoners behind me. I didn't know how much worse it would get for me until I marched further along.

There is nothing like the screams of a human being tortured, and it's something I'll never forget. I can still hear the cries of a group of about five or six Filipinos who had been tied to a hay stack as I marched by. I don't know what they did but the Japanese had tied them to the stack and then set it on fire. I could not bear to watch because I knew they were being burned alive. Oh, it was awful. As we would march, there were cane fields on the sides of the road. The guys were so hungry they couldn't hold back. They would make a dash for the cane fields and hope they could return. Some were shot on the way there and some were shot on the way back. There were a few that made it but I soon found out the risk was not worth it.

National Archives

Bataan Death March

National Archives   Proviso East Research Project

Bataan Death March

There are a lot of artisan wells in the Philippines that just flow freely out of the ground. As we marched we would pass those wells and some of the guys would make a dash for the water as they did for the cane fields. I tried it one time until a bullet went by my head so close, I could feel it. I jumped back into line and that was the end of my attempts at bravery. The Japanese guards that rode on horseback were ones that you had to keep an eye out for. If you were marching close to the outside and he took a swing at you with his sword, you had to duck or suffer the consequences. The Japanese officers did not seem to mind and I really felt like they encouraged it. Every once in a while, Filipinos who lived in the huts on the side of the road would try to give us food as we walked by, but if they were caught, they would be shot or bayoneted. The Japanese would even kill their babies with their bayonets and hold them up in the air to prove something. Those Filipinos were really brave for standing up to the Japanese and risking their lives. They would sometimes hide behind the banana trees and try to catch a straggler as he walked by. I don't what happened to them but I hoped they got fed. If you were lucky enough to get food and if the Japanese saw you, they would knock it out of your hands and everyone behind you would step on it. I had very little water or food for the entire march of seven days and ninety-six miles. On the fifth, sixth and seventh days, I had a spoonful of rice. One time I came across some candy of some sort. I don't even remember how I got it. I would imagine a Filipino threw it at us as we walked by and I caught it and put in my pocket to snack on.

National Archives

Bataan Death March

We stopped one night in a small town and were made to go into a small wooden shack. We were so cramped up in there it was horrible. We were made to back up against each other until no one else could get in. Then they told us to sit down with our knees up against our chest and that's the way we slept. There was another problem: We were not the first ones to sleep in that shack. Remember a lot of the guys including myself had dysentery. The floor was covered in feces from the prior group and that was what we had to sit in. There were a couple of guys who went crazy and the Japanese took them out. I don't know what happened to them but I never saw them again.

A funny thing happened to me on the march the next day. I was walking down the road talking to Eugene when I noticed that the guy in front of me kept looking back. I guess he was looking at all the guys behind him. He had a really heavy beard, more than an American, and I thought, "It can't be!" The next time he looked back we both looked right at each other and it hit both of us at the same time. We yelled "Rinky Dink!" That was the name of our Little League Baseball team back in Austin, Texas. His name was George Seyman and he was our catcher. His daddy owned a shoe repair shop on Red River Street, which was just around the corner from where we lived. He was an Arab, which explains the heavy beard growth. He moved away when he was fourteen, so I hadn't seen him since then. Just think, of all the guys on the march, I happened to be behind our old catcher from Austin, Texas. George, Eugene and I became real close buddies on this march and we looked out for each other. That was really important if we were to make it through this rough time. George was a medic and had some sulfathiazole tablets. Since I had dysentery real bad on this march, he gave me some and it cured me after a day or two.

That night, we had come to another town where we were to be put in a small shack again. This time we held back and were able to stay outside because it was too full. Since my dysentery was not completely healed, I had to go real bad. Everywhere I went, the ground was covered in human excrement, so it was hard to find a clean spot. On the march, you just went where you could and when you had a chance. There was no paper so you made do. On this night, there was a Filipino that was trying to make a little campfire. The Japanese guard had yelled at him to stop and put it out. He didn't want any camp fires. For some reason, he ignored the guard. While he was bent over making the fire, The Japanese Guard raised his rifle and plunged his bayonet right through his back and out the front. He pulled it out, wiped the blood off with a towel and just grinned, leaving him there to die. It was painful to watch, but there was nothing we could do. If we had tried to help, we would have been shot and killed ourselves.

National Archives

Bataan Death March

National Archives

Proviso East Research Project

Bayonet practice on a Filipino   **_Bataan Death March-192[nd]_**
Tnk Bn Co. A soldiers having
their possessions examined

Later on that night, they had tied an American prisoner to a tree and were beating him up pretty bad. I don't know what he had done, but they were hitting and slapping him and poking him with their bayonets. After he was tortured for some time, they took him down and shot him. The Japanese would also use prisoners for bayonet practice when they saw fit. They were always practicing with their swords and bayonets, as if to show us they were mightier than us. That's one thing that really got to me. They would use brutality and torture tactics as if to intimidate us. They had no regard for human life, especially those who had surrendered. They were exceptionally hard on those who were a lot taller than them, knowing there was nothing they could do in response. Some of the men who had fallen down were forced to dig their own graves and were knocked into it then buried alive. One of the terror tactics the Japanese would use was to have fallen soldiers' own comrades beat them until they got up or until they died. This was something I witnessed on numerous occasions during this march. They would also tie up prisoners to a fence post, slice them open until their intestines came out and then leave them there to die. The soldiers would be laughing the whole time as if it were just a game to them. They were brutal and inhumane beyond belief or comprehension.

This march was exceptionally hard on the older soldiers who were in their fifties and sixties. They were predominantly officers and were treated with no more respect than we were. They too would fall victim to the atrocities committed by the Japanese on the march. Rank did not matter, nor did the value of life as we know it.

Photo by Rick Peterson- www.bataansurvivor.com

San Fernando Train Station as it is today

We eventually ended up at the San Fernando train station where we were forced into boxcars that

57

were designed to hold about thirty men, but instead were crammed with about a hundred half-dead, diseased and starved prisoners. We were already beaten down from the Death March and then we had to go through this hell ride. We thought they would at least leave the doors open, but instead they closed them. When they closed the doors on us that heat became unbearable. Some of the prisoners tried to keep the doors open but they were hit with rifle butts and poked with bayonets. It was so packed in there that some of the men went crazy because they couldn't move. By the time we reached our destination, a few of the guys had died from the heat. They died standing because there was no room to fall. The tropical sun beat down on that boxcar and turned it into a broiler during the hottest month of the year in the Philippines. Temperatures in that boxcar felt like 130 degrees. Combined with the stench of human excrement as well as dead and crazed prisoners, the trip was unbearable. It was a long four- or five-hour trip over twenty-four miles to Capas where we got off of the train and marched another seven miles to Camp O'Donnell, which was our first camp. It felt good to get off the train, but I was so tired and weak I barely made it to the camp.

Camp O'Donnell

Camp O'Donnell was an old, abandoned, diseased-infested Philippine Army Post near Tarlac. It was around April 20th, 1942, when I arrived here. They had old rundown nipa huts with wooden posts holding them up. There was a rusty old barbed wire fence surrounding the camp and the weeds were waist high. With all the confusion, I lost contact with the two friends I had on the march and didn't know what happened to them. It was mass chaos from the time we got off the train. There was no sense of organization or leadership on any side. As soon as we entered the camp, we were ordered to stand at attention so we could be searched again and have all of our belongings we had left taken. After that, the Camp Commander, Captain Tsuneyoshi, ordered us to fall in formation so he could tell us what we could and could not do as prisoners. He had a huge sword hanging on his left side. He said, "You men are cowards! You should have committed suicide. You are lower than dogs and do not deserve to live. We will fight you until you have been destroyed. It is regrettable that we were unable to kill each of you on the battlefield. We do not consider you to be prisoners of war. You are members of an inferior race, and we will treat you as we see fit. We had nothing to do with the Geneva Convention. Whether you live or die is of no concern to us. If you violate any of the rules, you will be shot immediately. Your country has forgotten your name. Your loved ones no longer cry for you. You are the enemy of Japan. You men will soon find out that your dead comrades were the lucky ones! You will salute a Japanese soldier when you see him and bow when he talks to you." This speech went on for a couple of hours, and all the while he was screaming and hollering in Japanese with a translator telling us all of this in English. Quite a few guys passed out from the heat. We couldn't help them until the speech was over. It seemed like there was a few thousand POWs there at the time. As the train would unload POWs, the next group came in and heard the same speech. That was the first stop for the POWs, so eventually all the men who survived the march ended up there. By this time most of us were starved, emaciated, and had dysentery and cholera. There were a lot of guys who looked like walking skeletons.

Our only food there consisted of lugao, a watery soup made from old rotten rice and what ever else we could bargain for. We had no vitamins to offset the malnutrition, so beriberi was rampant, causing death among the POWs. There was a small stream, but it was scum-ridden and the latrines flowed into it, but some guys didn't care. Most of them died soon after drinking the water. I had learned on the march and in the months leading up to it how to discipline myself when drinking, and to never drink contaminated water, no matter how thirsty I was. I was not fortunate enough to get in a nipa hut. I slept on the ground at this camp, which in some ways was better. I could always move away from the really sick men.

Proviso East Research Project

Camp O'Donnell

National Archives

Camp O'Donnell Burial Detail

They had one old water spout in camp and the line to get a drink was about ten to twelve hours long. It seemed that guys were dying faster than it took to get a drink. There is an old saying: "Dying is easy, living is hell." That is true. I was put on the burial detail shortly after I got to camp. Approximately 16,000 died in the first two months at this camp. We would bury around a hundred guys a day. That was one of the most somber jobs I had as a POW. The smell of death was in the air and it was horrible. We would have to walk about two or three miles, carrying these dead soldiers to where we were going to bury them. Most were just bones with the skin barely hanging on. We would wake up in the mornings and find them dead by the latrines or already stacked up in a pile like firewood. When it would rain, the dirt would wash off and we would have to recover them in slushy mud. We had no tools for a proper hole, so we dug the best we could with our hands. Most of the time they were buried only a foot or two below the surface. I would always try to make a cross from sticks and hang their dog tags from it–if they had any. I did that job for a week and had all I could take. I was often dazed and exhausted and was not always aware of what was going on around me. It was definitely time to do something else.

At the first chance I had, I got on bridge building detail near Calauan, under the command of Captain Wakamori. We were reconstructing blown-up bridges so the Japanese could use all the roads for troop and supply movements. Some of the guys were sent back to Bataan to repair the U.S. trucks that were not destroyed and bring them back so they could be used. It was during my first detail that I contracted my first case of malaria. I was quarantined at the camp headquarters for a few days. Having malaria is not fun, and depending on the severity, it can kill you. I had a high fever and was constantly shivering and walked around in a blanket for two or three days. A large number of POWs died from malaria. We had it pretty good at this detail. Since we were far away from the main units and commanders, the captain in charge gave us more freedom. It was sure welcome considering what had happened to me and what I had witnessed so far. The guards would let the Filipino ladies give us a sweet vermicelli type of food while we were out on detail. It sure tasted good after having lugao and next-to-nothing for food so far. I also remember a German who had a plantation close by. The Japanese guards would let us take a bath and swim occasionally in the nearby stream. We had some fun with the guards as well. You know how some guys think they're the best in sports and athletics, well that was the Japanese. They would challenge us every chance they got. We had a lot of races with them but as always, the Americans would prevail. They even had an advantage in that they were healthier, but we still gave them a run for their money. They also let us play softball against the local Filipinos when time permitted. Well, good things must come to an end and I sure hated to leave. Although it was hard labor, the guards were great which helped ease some of the tension we had.

I had developed a huge sore on my left arm which encompassed the elbow area and could not work, so they transferred me to a town close to the sea with a name I can't remember. I was put in the kitchen as a cook's helper. It was at this camp where I put back on much-needed weight. I helped wash the cooking utensils and keep the kitchen clean. Since I did a good job, he would always give me some extra rice. We slept in a coconut factory, and needless to say, we managed to steal coconut meat and live off of that as well. I was transferred to Cabanatuan a few weeks later when Camp O'Donnell closed.

Cabanatuan

I arrived at Camp Cabanatuan around September 8th, 1942. This camp was made up of a number of nipa huts that looked almost like a small town. The guys gave some of the walkways names from cities back home. It was so crowded at this camp that we were shoulder-to-shoulder. There was no room to lay down comfortably when it was time to go to sleep. There were times when we, including myself, would desire the death of our fellow soldier lying next to us so that we would have more room to stretch out and sleep after a hard day's work in the dust fields. We started developing a farm outside of camp where we would go to work seven days a week, from sunup to sundown. Food, as always, was scarce except for the lugao the Japanese gave us. Occasionally, we would get some of the vegetables we harvested there at camp. The guards were so mean at this camp. If you stepped out of line slightly, or did not do the job how they wanted it done, you would get beaten down to the ground. Every once in a while you would find a nice Japanese guard who did not have the war spirit. A lot of the guards who were in these camps were the ones who could not make it onto the battlefield and were mentally unstable. The spare time we had at this camp was used to remove the lice off of our bodies. We wore the same clothing without a bath, day in and day out. Most of our clothes were rags by this time. There were some guys who had just a G-string, and others who had their feet sticking out of the front of their shoes because they were worn out. Our restroom was a slit trench near the back of our nipa hut and it was full of maggots. These maggots would crawl all over you while you were squatting down doing your business. The flies were unbearable there, due to the huge amount of maggots crawling all over the place. The stench of the trenches carried all the way through our huts where we slept making it difficult to sleep.

National Archives

Camp Cabanatuan

Ortega, Abel F. (23)
38029189
Bldg. No. 26
192nd Tank Bn.
8247
Artist
Private.
Mrs. Deborah Ortega
505 East 9th St.
Austin, Texas

POW card from Cabanatuan. My POW # is 8247

A lot of the prisoners just had ratty, old, torn clothes with their toes sticking out from their boots. Almost all of the prisoners had diseases like beriberi, which caused their bodies to swell, and yellow jaundice, which turned their bodies yellow. The prisoners were walking skeletons with bones protruding from the skin and eyes sunken back into their heads. Even those prisoners had to do their share of work.

After I had been there a while, the Japanese looked for prisoners who were physically fit enough to go to the other side of the road to the hospital ward—also known as "zero ward"—to guard the sick prisoners from trying to escape. The prisoners who went into the zero ward usually never came out. Approximately 1,400 died in the first two months at this camp, which is considerably less than at Camp O'Donnell. This wasn't really a hospital, because we had no medicine, proper facilities, or equipment to treat diseases that were rampant among the POWs. This is where I met up with my friend from Austin, Texas, Joel Ruiz. He had also volunteered to go work as a guard. We would eat together, stayed in the same hut and just tried to do everything together we could. Having someone I knew from my hometown made my stay there a little more comfortable.

It was horrible to see these guys this way, but there was nothing we could do. Those prisoners were so far gone, they could not think clearly. They would try to walk out of the camp or walk right into the fence. It was our job to make sure no one escaped. The Japanese would put the prisoners in ten-man groups, and if one of the prisoners escaped, they would shoot and kill the other nine. As always, there were guards in the building with us and in the towers to make sure we didn't slip away ourselves.

I saw a prisoner lying on the ground, barely alive, with his mind gone, and his body nothing but bone. I couldn't say "skin and bones" because there was hardly any skin left. Nearby would be another prisoner who was gravely ill, but still had a desire to eat, so he would try to find worms or frogs or anything close on the ground that moved. Next to him would be another prisoner who hadn't the strength to get up and use the bathroom, so he would go all over himself, with the stench that comes from it all. The whole camp smelled that way. This is what I saw and had to deal with on a daily basis. After they died, we had to bury them. This was a familiar work detail for me, but for others it was hard. There were other details that would dig holes all day because they knew there would always be prisoners dying. We would tie some tall grass (similar to our Johnson grass) around their wrists and ankles and pick them up. It usually took four of us—one on each arm and leg—to carry them to the little so-called cemetery a few miles away. Some days it would be hot and some days it would rain. In this part of the world they have monsoon seasons, so when it rains, it rains hard. We would have to carry the dead prisoners for about three miles to the little cemetery, crossing creeks and sloshing in the mud. When we got there, the hole would sometimes be filled with water, and all we could do was put the prisoner in the hole and scoop the slushy mud over his body. If he had dog tags we would put them on a stick by his head. There was not always enough time to completely bury the prisoners, or the rain would wash the dirt right off. Sometimes a leg or an arm would stick out, but we did the best we could. I buried a lot of fine American soldiers there and at Camp O'Donnell. And the next day it would start all over again. Those were sad days alright.

While at this camp I had developed hundreds of blisters in my mouth to the point where I lost all desire to eat. When I would try to eat the pain was so unbearable that I had to stop. I was rapidly losing weight. I could drink water but even that was painful. Because we had no medicine to cure this, it would not take long for me to die once I stopped eating. Were it not for my friend Joel and the Lord above, I probably would not be here today. He was like a mother to me while I was sick. He forced me to eat, so I could keep my strength up, even though it hurt.

I don't know how or where he got some lemons but he forced me to eat them raw. This went on for a few days and boy did it hurt. The acid from the lemons burned and burned. I finally got better and I thank God that Joel was there to help me through this.

You know I would never cut short the American art of ingenuity and survival. If there was ever any food available, leave it up to these prisoners of war to find a way to get it, by stealing, kniving, bribing, or even dying for it. By this time, we were starting to learn how to deal with the Japanese guards. We made many a deal with them, so that we could buy anything available from the Filipinos, like coconuts. This was how we learned the art of survival, because that's all we had to concern ourselves with. We had to survive by whatever means we had.

It was at this camp that I started to put my God-given talent to use, increasing my chances of survival. I carved prisoners' names or faces on their cups or on the sides of their canteens in exchange for a little extra salt, sugar or rice. I remember there were a few who wanted their sweethearts' names on their cups. I don't recall how many canteens and cups I designed for extra food. If you happened to find a pencil on the ground, it was like finding a gold mine. You could bargain for whatever you wanted with that pencil. There were a few prisoners who became good metal smiths and made their own eating utensils. No matter where we went, the food was always the same. It was a watery rice soup called Lugao. That was our main course every day. Some days it would be cooked a little more than others—and even burned. That's how we learned to make coffee. Since we did not have any actual coffee, we would burn the rice black then boil it in water. The water would come out black and that was our coffee. It was not as good as the mountain grown coffee, but that's all we had and we got used to it.

National Archives

Camp Cabanatuan

May 7, 1943

• Mrs. Deborah Ortega,
    505 East 9th Street,
    Austin, Texas.

Dear Mrs. Ortega:

The records of the War Department show your son, Private Abel F. Ortega, 38,029,189, Infantry, missing in action in the Philippine Islands since May 7, 1942.

All available information concerning your son has been carefully considered and under the provisions of Public Law 490, 77th Congress, as amended, an official determination has been made continuing him on the records of the War Department in a missing status. The law cited provides that pay and allowances are to be credited to the missing person's account and payment of allotments to authorized allottees are to be continued during the absence of such persons in a missing status.

I fully appreciate your concern and deep interest. You will, without further request on your part, receive immediate notification of any change in your son's status. I regret that the far-flung operations of the present war, the ebb and flow of combat over great distances in isolated areas, and the characteristics of our enemies impose upon some of us this heavy burden of uncertainty with respect to the safety of our loved ones.

Very truly yours,

J. A. ULIO
Major General,
The Adjutant General.

This was the letter that was sent to my grandmother in 1943 concerning dad's situation in the Philippines.

Lipa Batangas

I was eventually transferred to Lipa Batangas on January 28th, 1943. I would spend the longest time at this camp. Here, we mainly did airport and runway construction. All day, every day we would carry fifty pound sacks of cement on our backs and shoulders from the trains to the warehouse, then to the runways where the mixers were. We would then add the sand and gravel and pour the runways by hand. If there were big rocks in the way, we would have to bust them up with our picks and shovels. We also had to work in the gravel pits. When the day was over, we were always covered in a white powder that stuck to us because of the sweat. It was extremely hard and brutal work. The Japanese guards would hit and beat you down if you didn't pour the cement the right way or mix it exactly how they wanted. The food was always the same: lugao and more lugao. Every once in a while, we would get the green leaf tops from carrots and boil them with water to have "carrot top soup."

One day I was at the warehouse where we had our cement bags and I was approached by two fellow prisoners. They asked me if I would draw them a map of the Philippine Islands in exchange for extra food. I said I certainly would. Since I was known around camp as the artist, I was always drawing continuously for food so I never thought anything of it. We had a sailor in my barracks who had a map of the Philippines so I borrowed it. I made them a copy on one of the old cement bags we had there in the warehouse. I gave them the map and they gave me the extra food as promised. Well, you remember that compass I had hidden from the Japanese; I noticed it was gone a few days later. I had it just in case I escaped, so I would know what direction I needed to go in the jungles. I figured one of the prisoners in my barracks had found it and stole it so they could trade it for some food. A few days had gone by and one of the Japanese guards came over to me and said they wanted to see me in the Camp Commander's office. I walked into his office and proceeded to sit down on a chair in front of his desk. Well, that really upset the Commander. He said that the chair was no place for me to sit and that I was to kneel down on the floor in front of the desk. I complied with his request. At that point, thoughts started to run through my mind and one of them was death. I could not think of any reason why he would call me to his office and make me kneel down in front of him. He pulled out a brown piece of paper from his desk drawer and spread it out. He made me get up and identify the paper. It was the map I had drawn of the Philippine Islands for the two prisoners. He asked me if I had drawn it. At that point I realized that they were questioning me about their planned escape. In case he was unaware of who they were, I did not want to implicate them, so I hesitated for about a minute and did not give him an answer. He then reached down from his belt and pulled out a .45 pistol and laid it on his desk. He said if I didn't give him an answer that he was going to use that pistol on me. Well at this point in my life, I had been threatened and beaten so many times that I really didn't pay much attention to his threat and did not fear his pistol. I figured I probably should tell the truth, though, so that now matter what happened to me, I would know that I stood by my belief that you should never lie. That always leads to another lie and I did not want to complicate matters any more than they were. I told him I had made the map in exchange for some food, because I was hungry. I noticed that there was a bag with food, a knife and my compass. They were the supplies needed in case they made their escape. After the Commander figured I was telling the truth, he let me go. Later that afternoon, I saw the two prisoners being escorted into the office. Later, they were loaded up on a truck and driven out of the camp. We didn't see them for about two weeks when they came back dirty and unshaven. I didn't see them after that, so I never knew what happened to them. After the war, I heard that they survived and made it back to the States, so I was happy about that.

After this failed escape attempt, the guards set up machine guns around the perimeter and put us in ten-man squads. If one of us escaped, then the other nine would be shot and killed. Just like Camp Cabanatuan. The guards were nervous. They were mostly young soldiers, since the older ones were out fighting the war. They called us out one day and cut our daily rations of food to where we really had nothing. They also took away our blankets that they had given us because it would get really cold at night. They tried to make it hard on us by taking our blankets and food. It didn't really matter, because we were used to not having much for warmth and we were always starving. We somehow managed to survive. I imagine they thought the whole compound was getting ready to escape.

Just a few months later, there was another escape attempt. This time it was the shoemaker and his assistant. I knew the assistant, whose name was House, because he was from my hometown of Austin, Texas. I lived on 9th Street and he lived in the house behind us. They made it out and we never saw them again. It was not until I came back home after the war that I saw him again. I was walking down Congress Avenue when I saw an Army Recruiter named Sergeant House. I went up to talk to him but he just turned away and would not speak to me. I assume it was because he thought the other men in his ten-man squad were executed because of his escape. If he would have talked to me I could have told him that they did not execute the other eight. Instead, they put them on heavy work details and cut their rations. I just kept on going letting him think that he caused the death of the other eight soldiers that were in his group. It would be something on his mind for rest of his life.

We started to alternate our work from the runways to the farm fields where we planted beans. At this detail, if we did our fair share of work, the guards would let us have the last thirty minutes to ourselves to pick some of the beans to eat. The best way to carry the beans was in your shirt sleeve. You would tie the cuff in a knot and put the beans down the sleeve. Some of the guys used small bags, but the shirt worked the best. We would build a small fire at camp and cook the beans. Although we never got full, we managed to add a little extra substance to our meals. It helped keep our strength up and, thanks to God; I was always able to do my fair share of work. We would always manage to give some of the beans to the POWs at camp who were too sick to work, and give them a little hope of survival.

One of the Japanese guards in charge of my detail subjected Lieutenant Wandell to an extremely brutal beating. One day we had been sent out on a work detail on an airstrip and it was Lieutenant Wandell's duty to go with the truck. This Japanese guard did not like Lieutenant Wandell and was looking for a chance to abuse him. For a reason not clear to me, he took this occasion to abuse the Lieutenant. When the work was complete, about twenty of us, including Lieutenant Wandell, were retained and made to stand at attention in formation. Four armed guards with loaded rifles were placed at each end of the formation. Lieutenant Wandell was ordered to report to the rear of the formation and told to assume a "push-up" position. The guard then pulled out his pistol and a big stick and began to beat him across the back and legs. This continued until Lieutenant Wandell began to sink from pain and exhaustion. When he finally fell to the ground, the guard beat him even harder until he got off the ground and back into the "push-up" position. The Lieutenant could see us starting to move towards the guards but yelled at us to stop. He was a tough Texas boy. This lasted for about ten minutes, until the guard had had enough satisfaction in beating him and finally allowed him to rise. He was staggering and had become very weak after the beating, so we helped him. I believe that this so far was the closest that my fellow soldiers and I had come to an outbreak of resistance. When they had first lined us up, they forgot to take away our picks and shovels. We were getting ready to attack the guard and even take his life when Lieutenant Wandell called us off.

During another one of our work details, there was this Japanese guard who always loved to shadowbox with his sword. He would walk up and down the rows, trying to find someone who would challenge him to a match. As Americans, we never did any kind of sword fighting growing up, so we did not truly understand the techniques. He knew that and kept on insisting that someone challenge him. We all finally got tired of him so we said, "Will someone go out there and just hold a stick or something so he'll quit?" Someone finally stepped up and the guard was happy. He put up his real sword and cut two sticks about the size of a sword so they could fight. The guard tried to scare the prisoner by giving a loud "Banzai!" Since the prisoner was used to the yelling, he was not scared. Because he didn't know how to sword fight, he just stuck up his sword and leveled it off. To the disgrace of the Japanese guard, the stick went right into his mouth. The Japanese guard was caught by surprise, but not as much as the prisoner, who didn't even know how to sword fight. The guard didn't know what to say, so the prisoner humbly went back to work and never looked back, just in case the guard wanted to beat him for humiliating him in front of us. We were just glad that he would finally leave us alone.

By this time we had learned the Japanese language enough to converse with them and to march according to their commands. It made it easier, because we could finally understand what to do when they ordered us.

Camp Murphy

I was transferred to Camp Murphy on March 26th, 1944. It was an old Philippine Army Base that had been converted to a POW camp. Again we engaged in airport runway building, but there were not any runways, so we had to start from scratch. So life began to emerge as it did with all the other camps, but now it was easier to communicate since we were able to understand them. We learned quickly which guards we could build a relationship with, since they were not all brutal. At this camp we learned to wheel and deal with the outside population so we could get more food into camp. As I have said before, American ingenuity never falters when you are trying to survive. The Japanese would let us eat coconuts here, but we had to eat them on the details and couldn't bring them into camp. There were a few of us who learned how to smuggle them in by breaking them up and putting them in shirt sleeves or in small bags that were tied to our bodies. We also made arrangements with the outside people to smuggle them in when they came to camp in their water buffalo-drawn wagons. We all learned to steal any way we could to survive.

One of the things we always did when we went to a new camp was to scout out the food in the area. We looked around camp and on the trip to and from work details. Our only means of finding out if it was edible was for someone to try it. If they got sick, we didn't eat it. If they were OK, then we ate it. We would look for any type of seeds, beans, plants, roots and whatever else looked edible, along with leaves to make tea.

At this camp there was Japanese guard who was mentally unstable. The Camp Commander let him harass us any way he could. If one of the guards did not like you, they would send you to his detail. I was already on his detail and it was horrible. He would have us out on the runway putting rocks down, and then he would come behind us and make us turn the rocks a certain way. He was never satisfied with the shape of any rock or how we put it down. We would turn it one way and he did not like it. We would turn it another way and he did not like it. Everything was wrong. He would hit us on the head or back and make us keep turning it. He never seemed to know which way he wanted it. He would go from one prisoner to another, hitting us, and never making any sense. It was pure harassment, and it made our days go by slowly. We had to have good control over ourselves in situations like this. There were many times the thought ran through my mind to pick up a rock and just hit him over the head and do away with him but I had to get rid of those thoughts if I were to survive. We would dig holes in solid rock by hand for dynamite to blast them. We would then have to carry the rocks over to the trucks and load them up so they could be hauled to the runway and used for the base. By this time, we had no shoes and were barefoot. The years and months of hard labor had taken its toll on our shoes. When our feet got cut, all we could do was walk over to a muddy pit and wash them off the best we could.

It was at this camp where I was punished severely. One morning, two POWs and I were late for roll call and falling into formation. The Japanese guard walked past us, slapping the side of our faces with the flat part of his bayonet. He then turned around and slapped us on the other side of the face, trying to knock us down. When we did not fall, he ordered us to kneel down on the ground in a row. He then placed a stick about two to three inches in diameter with the sharp short pieces of the limbs still sticking out against the back of our legs at the knee joint. He ordered us to rock back onto the sticks. Later he walked by, hitting us in the face with his fist trying to break us. When he got bored, he started to jump on our thighs, forcing the sticks further into the backs of our legs and calves. This punishment lasted about twenty minutes and was very painful. I wasn't late after that.

By early September of 1944, we had not heard any news of the war except from the Japanese, who said we were conquered and would be under Japanese rule. All we saw were Japanese planes and vehicles. Our clothes were down to G-strings and ratty old Japanese uniforms that did not fit since they were much shorter than us. Our situation looked like it was getting worse with no end in sight. Well, one day we got our first glimmer of hope. The Japanese had started making us build U-shaped embankments to park the planes in case they were bombed. We had quite a few built when one day we looked up and saw two Japanese planes doing target practice, which was quite common. One plane had a target being towed behind it, while the other plane shot at it. All of a sudden, we heard a low humming noise that started to get louder and louder. We looked up and saw a formation overhead which consisted of bombers and fighters. We thought they were Japanese until we saw a few of the fighters break formation and head for the two planes doing target practice. Boy they let them have it and we thought they were shooting at their own countrymen. Then one of the planes flew down low and we could see a white star on the bottom of the plane. We all started jumping for joy as the two Japanese planes crashed to the ground as American planes flew over. What a great feeling that was. Then they started to strafe the camp not knowing POWs were down there. But you know we didn't care. We were jumping up and down with such joy while they were shooting. It was great to finally see some American planes. That's when we knew the Americans were getting close. The Japanese made us get into the ditches and holes and whatever safe place they could find. The American planes shot up the buildings and planes on the ground, so there was not much left for us to do at that camp. The Japanese guards got orders to move us out, so we left soon after that by truck for Bilibid Prison.

Bilibid Prison

On September 21st, 1944, 363 Americans, including myself, arrived at Bilibid Prison in Manila. This was an old prison built a long time ago by the Spaniards. I did not do much at this prison except walk around and keep to myself. There was a Spaniard civilian the Japanese soldiers did not bother who would come in and out of the prison. Since I spoke Spanish, I had spoken to him a few times, and one day he asked if I wanted to escape. He said he could sneak me out through the yard and would have no problems on the outside. I thought about it for a while but decided to stay with my fellow soldiers and keep the promise to God I made at the surrender. That was all the excitement I had here. We only stayed there for about a week and a half before we marched down to the docks to be loaded onto the Hell Ship that was supposed to take us to Japan after detouring to Formosa. We got to the docks October 1st, 1944, and boarded the ship.

Rick Peterson- www.bataansurvivor.com

Bilibid Prison

Roger Mansell

Bilibid Prison

National Archives

Bilibid Prison in 1944 at the time of the Philippine Liberation

Hell Ship Description

I want you to try and imagine you have been forced into the dark, rocking hold of a ship in the Pacific Ocean. The tropical sun beats down mercilessly. There is no cool, soft breeze to alleviate the intense heat. You get nothing but a scoop of rice to eat and a canteen of water to drink if you are lucky. You are packed in with many men so tightly, there is hardly any room to sit or lie down. Madness and insanity are common among those around you. If you are suffering from dysentery or malaria, there is no medicine to treat you. Bathroom facilities consist of a bucket shared by all the men. You have no way of knowing if you will ever see your home or family again and you are only twenty-five years old. Welcome to Hell on Earth... You are on board a WWII Japanese prisoner of war ship called a "Hell Ship."

The term "Hell Ship" has been used to refer to the ships the Japanese used to move POWs to various camps during World War II. Contrary to the provisions of the Geneva Convention, these ships were not marked in any way to show that they were transporting POWs. Many were targeted by U.S.

submarines and aircraft and attacked with great loss of life to POWs held by the Japanese.

The Japanese were also notorious for the completely inhumane way that prisoners were crowded into cargo holds with no ventilation and only minute amounts of water and food—sometimes none for days. During the transport of POWs in the area of the Philippine Islands during the summer following the infamous Bataan Death March, the temperatures in the cargo holds rose above 110 degrees, causing many POWs to become insane from the intense heat. Then, in January 1945, as the last of these ships approached Japan, temperatures were well below freezing. Most POWs were wearing only a khaki shirt and shorts. Some had only a G-string, causing many to freeze to death.

It is hard for people in today's society to really understand or grasp what the American and Allied prisoners of war under the Japanese Command went through on these Hell Ships. I wish there was a way to put into words what really happened in the dark and damned underworld of a Japanese Hell Ship cargo hold, but there isn't. In talking with my father, I can tell that there are a lot of things that happened on those Hell Ships that he doesn't want to talk about. Some things has he been able to mention only recently. He told me that the 39 days he spent on the first Hell Ship were the worst that he would ever experience as a prisoner of war. I can only speculate that when a human mind is subjected to such inhumane conditions and unspeakable atrocities, it blocks certain experiences and goes into a survival mode, causing them to shut out painful recollections. The resilience and will to survive that the POWs had on those Hell Ships is truly amazing to me. I don't think that we will ever comprehend what they went through. Incredibly, some went through those conditions two or three times. There were prisoners on ships that were sunk, recaptured and put aboard another ship, which was sunk again. Some survived, but many did not. A majority of the prisoners had already spent two and a half years in various prison camps before being put aboard a Hell Ship. It is truly sad to have survived the beatings and tortures for two and a half years, and then be put aboard a Hell Ship, only to be killed by friendly fire because the ships were unmarked. More than 126,000 Allied Prisoners were transported in Hell Ships, and more than 21,000 died. Of those 21,000 fatalities, approximately 19,000 were caused by friendly fire from Allied submarines or planes.

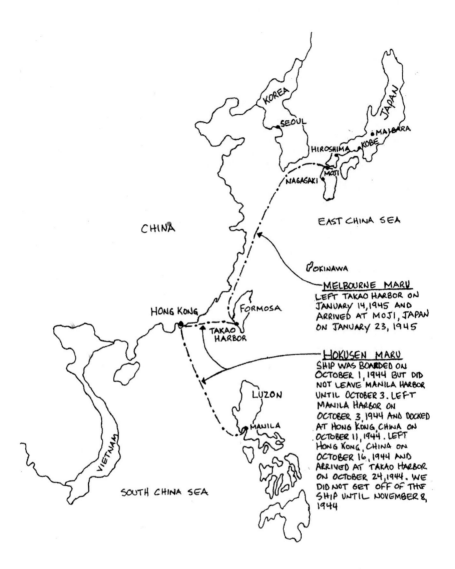

KOREA

SEOUL

JAPAN

HIROSHIMA KOBE MAIBARA

NAGASAKI MOJI

CHINA

EAST CHINA SEA

OKINAWA

HONG KONG FORMOSA

TAKAO HARBOR

MELBOURNE MARU
LEFT TAKAO HARBOR ON
JANUARY 14, 1945 AND
ARRIVED AT MOJI, JAPAN
ON JANUARY 23, 1945

HOKUSEN MARU
SHIP WAS BOARDED ON
OCTOBER 1, 1944 BUT DID
NOT LEAVE MANILA HARBOR
UNTIL OCTOBER 3. LEFT
MANILA HARBOR ON
OCTOBER 3, 1944 AND DOCKED
AT HONG KONG, CHINA ON
OCTOBER 11, 1944. LEFT
HONG KONG, CHINA ON
OCTOBER 16, 1944 AND
ARRIVED AT TAKAO HARBOR
ON OCTOBER 24, 1944. WE
DID NOT GET OFF OF THE
SHIP UNTIL NOVEMBER 8,
1944

LUZON

MANILA

VIETNAM

SOUTH CHINA SEA

PACIFIC
OCEAN

92

REGULATIONS FOR PRISONERS

Commander of P.O.W. Escort
Navy of the Great Japanese Empire

    The prisoners disobeying the following orders will be punished with immediate death:

I.   a.   Those disobeying orders to instructions.

     b.   Those showing a motion to antagonism by raising a sign of opposition.

     c.   Those disobeying the regulations by individualism egoism, thinking only about yourself or rushing for your own good.

     d.   Those talking without permission and raising loud voices.

     e.   Those walking and moving without orders.

     f.   Those who carry unnecessary baggage in disembarking.

     g.   Those resisting mutually.

     h.   Those touching the boats material, wires, lights, tools, switches, et

     i.   Those showing action of running away from the room or boat.

     j.   Those climbing the ladder without permission.

     k.   Those taking more meal than given him.

     l.   Those using more than blankets.

II.   Since the boat is not well equipped and inside being narrow, food being scarce and poor you'll feel uncomfortable during the escort time on the boat. Those losing patience and disordering the regulations will be punished for the reason of not being able to escort.

III. Be sure to finish "nature's call". Evacuate the bowels and urine before embarking.

IV. Meal will be given twice a day. One plate only to one prisoner. the prisoners called by the guard will give out meal as quick as possible and honestly. The remaining prisoners will stay in their places quietly and wait for your plate. Those moving from their places, reaching for your plate without order will be heavily punished. Same orders will be applied to handling plates after meal.

V.   Toilet will be fixed in four corners of the room. the buckets and cans will be placed, when filled up a guard will appoint a prisoner. The prisoner called will take the buckets to the center of the room. The buckets will be pulled up by the derrick to be thrown away. Toilet paper will be given. Everyone must co-operate to make the sanitary. Those being careless will be punished.

VI. The navy of the Great Japanese Empire will not try to punish you all with death. Those obeying all rules and regulations and delivering the action and purpose of the Japanese Navy; co-operating with Japan in constructing the "New Order of the Greater Asia" which leads to the world peace will be well treated. The Great Japanese Empire will rise to Govern the World.

                END

Harrison Heritage ADBC

This is a document from the Japanese pertaining to the treatment and transportation of POWs during WWII on the "Hell Ships."

Hokusen Maru

I would spend thirty-nine days aboard the Hell Ship Hokusen Maru. Those thirty-nine days were the worst I would ever experience as a POW. It was hell on earth from the beginning. I was put in the forward cargo hold of the ship with about 500 other men. Since the hold had been carrying coal before our trip, the floor was covered in coal particles and dust. It was about forty-five feet by forty-five feet. We were so cramped in there that there was no room to move, yet the Japanese guards kept poking at us with their rifle butts and clubs until we were crammed in. There was no sense of reality. I was thinking that this could not be happening to me. The temperature in there was unbearable. Due to the heat of Manila, combined with the overcrowded conditions, men were passing out, and some were starting to go insane. It felt like it was at least 110 degrees in there with hardly any ventilation. It was as if I was having a horrible nightmare that I could never wake up from.

For the first couple of nights, no one got any sleep until a few men tied their blankets to the bulkheads and made crude hammocks. There was an American officer in our cargo hold named Major Farris, but he could not do anything to keep matters under control. In that type of situation, rank did not matter. None of us actually believed that this was how we were going to be transported, even though we did not know where we were going. People were stepping and tripping over each other, and that just added to the already insane and demoralizing conditions. There was no room to lie down unless you were to lie on top of someone else, so you either stood up or knelt down. There were men in a daze without any signs of life. When you would look at them, it was as if they were looking right through you. Other men would yell, scream, and cry. One minute, they would be alive, and then the next thing you knew, they were dead.

The nighttime was really hard on some of the guys because you could hardly see what was going on around you. When you would try to sleep, the screaming and moaning would keep you awake. The Japanese guards would threaten to shoot into the hold if we did not silence them. Some of the other POWs were forced to quiet them for fear the guards would shoot us. I am sure that's how a few of the POWs died. The rest would die from the heat, starvation, and lack of medical attention.

I would see guys scratching at the hull of the ship, trying to get out to the water. I don't know what they were doing, but it was awful to watch. We had a water bucket that was lowered to us where we would get about a half of a cup of water to fill our canteens, cups or whatever we had. We would also get a food bucket lowered to us that had small amounts of rice balls. Even if we were lucky enough to get either one, it wasn't enough to keep us going. Our restroom facilities consisted of a few five gallon buckets shared by all the men. They were called "benjo" buckets, which in Japanese means "toilet."

This Hell Ship had a nickname. It was called the Benjo Maru because we were in a forty-five foot by forty-five foot toilet for thirty-nine days. Most guys never got a chance to use the bucket, so they just went where they stood. When the bucket got full, we had to climb a ladder to take it topside and empty it. In the physical condition we were in, a lot of the guys could not hold the bucket. Sometimes the Japanese guards would raise it with a rope but the rope would break, and it just spilled on the guys below. Many of the POWs broke out with sores all over their bodies, and these would become infected from the overfilled benjo buckets splashing on them. There was no medical attention given to these guys, so they did not last long. Men were already sick from all different kinds of diseases. There are no words to describe the horrific smell. A lot of the guys could not hold their bowels, so they just went where they stood. We were standing, squatting and sleeping in excrement.

One good thing about the coal dust is that it helped absorb the excrement. Men were ill with malaria, diarrhea, dysentery, and beriberi and that's what caused a lot of them to go out of their minds. They would be screaming from one side of the hold to the other. Some would be kicking those men around them making it a living hell in the overcrowded conditions.

We boarded the ship on October 1st, 1944, but did not leave Manila until October 3rd. We sat in the

Harbor for three days. They finally put canvas and boards with chains over the cargo hold to keep the noise down. Well, that only made it worse. We suffered through thirty-nine days of stench, craziness, death, and starvation. Once we were underway, we could hear the ships in our convoy get hit with torpedoes, and that sent a lot of guys off their rocker. One torpedo passed so close that some of the guys heard it go right past us and hit the ship nearby. The force of the explosion rocked us from side-to-side so violently that we thought we were going to capsize. We had a few Navy guys in our hold so they could hear the sonar from the submarines and tell us when they were close. Men were starting to fend for themselves by stealing canteens and food whenever the opportunity arose by this time.

Because of the air raids on Formosa, we had to detour over to Hong Kong for a few days. We got there on October 11th and stayed there for about five days. During those days, I was fortunate enough one time to make it topside and use the outside benjo, which consisted of a plank of wood with a hole cut out that hung over the railing. I was right in the middle of my business when planes attacked us. I'm not sure if they were British or American planes, but they sure ruined my one time topside and almost cost me my life. I dove behind a small wall as the bullets strafed around me and ricocheted by my head. I finally got up when it was over and had to go back down into the hell hole. My only time topside during the thirty-nine days was cut short.

We finally left Hong Kong on October 16th. We eventually arrived at Formosa on October 24th, but did not get off the ship until November 8th. During our thirty-nine days at sea, we ended up throwing thirty-nine dead POWs overboard. When men died, we just had to throw them overboard, because there was no time for a burial. The devastating journey took one POW for every day at sea. While we were sitting in the harbor at Takao, Formosa, waiting to debark, there were two survivors from a Hell Ship, Arisan Maru, which had been sunk on October 24th put aboard our ship. One of the survivors was Glen Oliver. He was put right next to me and we got to talk about what had happened on his ship. I had a childhood friend named Joel Ruiz who belonged to the 200th CA who was on the Arisan Maru. I asked Glenn if he knew him and he did. He told me that he did not make it and I was very sad to hear that.

We finally debarked on November 8th. It was great to get off that ship and onto dry land. That trip will be stamped in my mind as the most horrible experience that any human being should ever have to endure. The overcrowded conditions, the heat, the stink, the thirst, the hunger, the misery and the screams of the men going out of their minds cannot be described with true understanding. Words alone cannot describe the horror of this journey.

But let me tell you how I believe my mother's prayers helped me through this journey. She spent many a night on her knees praying for her son's safety. Before I boarded the Hell Ship, I was walking up to get on and noticed on the edge of the dock a small can a POW had made. I heard a voice say, "Pick it up!" I looked around, but no one was talking to me. I heard it again: "Pick it up!" So I picked up the can and got on board. After I was shoved into the forward cargo hold, I landed where there was a funnel that brought in some air right above me. When it rained outside or condensation dripped, I would use this can to catch the water and trade it for extra rice when I could. That just goes to show you how the power of prayer can work for you in times of need. I know now it was God who told me to pick up that can.

Sometimes the mind tries to find a little humor in all bad situations as a coping mechanism. The floor of the hold was covered in coal dust, which made for a very dusty situation. It didn't matter what color you were going in, you were the same coming out. One guy would turn to another and say, "You look like me." Another would do the same, and then another and before you knew it, we were all laughing because Anglos and Mexicans all looked alike. There was no difference and to some of us, that was funny!

北 鮮 丸

Thore Kibsgaard

Hokusen Maru

The Hokusen Maru was a 2,256-ton freighter that had been used to haul coal and horses prior to dad boarding the ship. They were part of a convoy called Mata Twenty-eight that left Manila October 3rd, 1944. The convoy consisted of eight transport ships, three of which were sunk: the Hokurei Maru (sunk October 6th by Submarine Cabrilla SS-288), Shinyo Maru (sunk October 7th by Submarine Cabrilla SS-288), and Kohoku Maru (sunk October 7th by Submarine Hoe SS-258). Surviving the attacks were the Fumiyama Maru, Syoei Maru, Hokusen Maru, Terukuni Maru, and Hisigata Maru. It also consisted of three Escorts, Mine Sweepers #20 and 41, Sub-Chaser #41, and Tanker #2 Yamamizu Maru (sunk October 6th by Submarine Cabrilla SS-288).

The Captain of the Hokusen Maru was Tomiichi Tsutsui. Others in the crew were Chief Mate Kojiro Kamata, Chief Engineer Shozo Minato, Purser Shinsuke Yoshino, Chief Wireless Operator Tadashige Yamagata, and Guard Commander Lieutenant Kaseno.

Camp Toroku, Formosa

After we got off the ship at Takao Harbor on November 8, we did stevedore work on the docks for a few days. We were then marched to Camp Shirakawa #6 where we boarded a train that took us to Camp Toroku, which is located in the interior of Formosa. I arrived there around the 15th of November. The Camp Commander was Wakasugi. The others were Executive Officer Nokamura, First Sergeant Kohiga, Tech Sergeant Susuki, Staff Sergeant Hitomoto, and the Interpreter, Matsumoto.

We stayed in an old school close to a sugar mill, not far from the town of Toroku. The camp consisted of native-frame buildings with tile roofs and cement floors. We had a latrine at the end of the second row barracks. There were five barracks in each row. We also had a galley, a bathhouse, a washroom and a sick bay. There was a river about a quarter mile away that we sometimes used for baths. The camp was about a hundred square yards in size with a split-type bamboo fence surrounding it. Some guys worked at the sugar mill, some worked in town, and some worked on the farm. At the farm where I worked, I did the planting and fertilizing of the vegetables by emptying the "Honey Buckets" over the crops. Honey Buckets are tubs filled with excrement from the latrines after they were cleaned. The contents of the honey buckets caused the vegetables to grow faster and bigger than normal. A lot of the guys would eat some of the vegetables before they were ripe because they were so hungry, but would leave just enough so that the guards could not notice. Our food consisted of rice, grain and a fair share of vegetables. After doing that for a while, I had hurt my elbow. The Japanese didn't let me go to work so I would go to the kitchen and help clean up. I got in real good with the cook so he would give me some extra rice and carrot tops which let me put on some badly needed weight.

I was only at this camp for two months, so a lot did not happen to me there. There were the usual beatings and slapping around but nothing too serious. The Japanese were a lot nicer at this camp because they may have known that the war was going to be over soon. I don't really know. I remember a time when we were coming back from a work detail, we passed up a plant that had some beans that were in a pod. The plant was red with some flower buds in them. They looked just like pinto beans to us, so we all took a bunch back to camp with us. Along the way a couple of us decided to eat a few of them. By the time we got back to camp we were in pretty bad shape. I ate only a few and felt woozy, but the guys who ate more were worse off. We were just a bunch of city boys who didn't know any better. There were some old farmers there in camp and they told us that where they came from, those beans killed horses. We learned our lesson the hard way. We left Camp Toroku around January 8th, 1945, and took a train back to Shirakawa #6. We were then marched back to Takao Harbor where we boarded another Hell Ship called the Melbourne Maru, bound for Moji, Japan. We left Takao Harbor on January 14th, one day before Allied aircraft bombed the harbor area and docks.

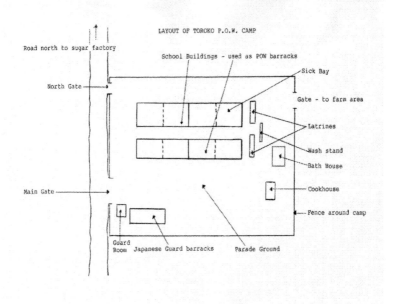

Drawing of Camp Toroku

Both pictures are courtesy of POWTAIWAN.ORG

Map of Formosa

The Hell Ships Brazil Maru and Enoura Maru left San Fernando, La Union, Luzon on December 27, 1944 and arrived at Takao Harbor, Formosa on December 31, 1944. On January 6, 1945, the surviving POWs from both ships were combined on the Enoura Maru. This photo of Takao Harbor was taken by aircraft from the USS Hornet during their bombing attack on January 9, 1945. Of the two ships at the lower right that appear to be burning, the Enoura Maru is the one closest to the pier. This bombing killed about 300 POWs on the Enoura Maru. The smallest ship of the three ships at the pier is probably the Brazil Maru. The Enoura Maru was too badly damaged for further sailing. All surviving Pows from the January 9th attack were moved to the Brazil Maru about January 13, 1945 and it sailed for Japan on January 14, 1945.

National Archives

107

National Archives

This photo is of the bombing of Takao Harbor on January 15, 1945 by Allied Aircraft. The ship docks are on the top right and are on fire from the Allied bombings. This bombing took place the day after dad left the harbor for Moji, Japan. The Americans had just about re-taken the Philippines and were moving closer to Formosa. In fact, the Japanese had ordered us to leave Camp Toroku due to the bombings.

Melbourne Maru

We left Takao Harbor on January 14th, 1945 for Moji, Japan. We had a lot more room on this ship compared to the first one we were on from Manila. Although the extra room was nice, it was still insufferable. We were only on this ship for nine days, and that helped.

After a few days on the ship, another fellow POW and I decided to climb down the sides of the ship's ribs when no one was looking to investigate what else was on board below in the cargo holds since it was such a big ship. It was dark down there so it took us a while for our eyes to adjust. After they did, we saw two guys guarding something and at the same time they were eating it. They had found a hidden treasure before we did. A slight scuffle came about because they did not want us to have any. We tried to be quiet so no one would hear us, but when you're hungry, you don't care. When we finally made our way through them, they gave up the struggle so we would not be caught. The treasure we had fought for was canned tomatoes, and they sure tasted good. It was like finding gold. We put some in our sleeves and pants' pockets and made our way back up to where we were supposed to be. We tried to be really quiet and not make any noise opening them up but you know, you can't keep a secret from a bunch of starving POWs. You could hear a "clang, clang, clang" all over the area. Evidently, others had found the tomatoes too and were dropping the cans down the sides of the ship when they were done. Nothing else worth mentioning happened on this trip. I don't think anyone died on the nine day trip. We finally arrived in Moji on January 23rd, 1945.

Japanese Merchant Ships at War

Melbourne Maru

The Melbourne Maru was a 5,438-ton passenger-cargo ship that was used primarily before the war to carry wool from Australia to Japan. When the war started, it was requisitioned by Japan. It was part of Convoy TAMO-37 that included the Brazil Maru, Oei Maru, and Hoshi Maru. The Captain of the Melbourne was Mitsuru Suganuma, and the crew included Chief Mate Sukahiro Morimoto and Purser Fumito Nakao.

Wakinohama Camp

We arrived in Moji, Japan, on January 23rd, 1945, and it was a shock. We had come from a warm tropical climate to bitter cold and snow. We had no winter clothes, just the shorts and shirts from the last camp, so when we left the cargo hold where it was warm, the cold air hit me like a rock. We assembled on an open area by the docks, and there was a little rain with sleet. I started to shiver and knew I was catching a cold right away so I grabbed a blanket that was on the ground and put it around me for warmth. When I started walking towards the train, Japanese guards made me leave the blanket. They did not care if you were freezing or not. We got on the train and started to head for Kobe-Osaka, Japan. They made us pull down the shades so we could not see where we were going. We arrived at Kobe-Osaka on February 12th, 1945, and went to a primary school on the docks of Kobe City. Kobe-Osaka are two cities right next to each other and are comprised mostly of steel mills and shipping docks. The address was 3 Chrome, Wakinohama-cho, Fukiai-ku, Kobe City, Japan. There were approximately 197 American, English, Australian and Dutch prisoners. They all came from Formosa. The Camp Commander's name was Captain Kazuo Takenaka. The Japanese civilian guards were Takee Kanamaru, Shigee Nagano, Iga Sadao.

Shortly after we arrived, we were given clean, but old, Japanese uniforms, a coat and a straw mat to sleep on. The platforms where we slept were side by side. We were finally permitted to take a bath. It had been two months since my last one in Formosa.

National Archives

Wakinohama Camp

National Archives

Wakinohama Camp

We were not far from the docks, which were about a mile away. We did hard-labor work for the Kawasaki Steel Mill Co. We would off-load trains that had scrap iron onto horse-drawn carts and take them to barges on the docks. On more than one occasion, I saw German Sailors loading supplies onto small ships just a few blocks down. Since they were allies with the Japanese, they could do that. Japanese civilians would come by with old junk cars, bikes and whatever they had and we had to load that on the barges, as well. Every once in a while we would get to work in the warehouses that stored grain. That would be the best working detail I had.

113

I was finally working around food. For three years I had been starving, so this was a blessing. We even had to load for the Japanese soldiers that came by in trucks who wanted some grain or food. We would end up sneaking some grain for ourselves too. We would put it in small Bull Durham tobacco sacks that we would tie under our arm pits and other places so the Japanese guards back at camp would not see it. One day we were done with our work and standing in formation to go back. This time everyone was loaded down. The Japanese guard in charge of our detail did not care if we had the sacks and kept quiet about it until that day. The Camp Commander was walking towards us as we were getting ready to leave and the guard saw him. He told us to go behind this building quickly to get rid of the small sacks and get back into formation. We ran around the building and started to fling the sacks up on the small roof tops but some of them got hung up on the power and telephone lines. We were all sweating it, hoping that he would not look up and see the bags swinging on the lines. A few of them fell and hit the ground. That was a close call, but thanks to God and the guard, we were saved from punishment that day. We were able to get some of those sacks back though and continue our trades. We even had our own way of communicating with the main camp when we were on the docks. Since our camp was a three story building, we could see the top floor windows from the warehouses and docks. We had a designated window we used on the top floor. If it was all the way open, then it was safe to bring things back. If it was halfway shut, we had to be cautious. If it was closed, forget it.

Since there were so many of us at that camp, we were all on different details. The ones who did not have the dock detail didn't have access to the food that we did. We would sneak food back into the camp and trade it for other things we needed. When we would go to work on the docks, the cook would come with us and set up his kitchen in a small shack at the warehouse complex. If we had come across some corn that day, he would make popcorn for us to eat. Since the Japanese only gave us a small spoonful of rice a day, we would sneak some extra rice to the cook so he would add it to the daily rations. The cook also had a pet dog that ran around the kitchen. One day someone said were having meat with our soup. We said, "Meat? We never have meat." Well, when we got our soup it was only a couple of slivers. We later found out someone had added the dog to our soup when the cook wasn't looking, and he was mad.

We were always trying to find ways to improve our living conditions, food sources and our clothes. You see, every time we went to a new camp or work detail, we would scout out the area for whatever we could use. At this camp, we constantly sent out spies to look in the different warehouses for things we needed and could sneak back into camp. We would have a couple of lookouts and a couple of guys doing the scouting. One day, we were checking out another warehouse and we came across some large bolts of cloth. We thought to ourselves, we could sure use some new under shorts. Some of us didn't have any and those that did had G-strings under the ratty old pants the Japanese gave us. The G-string was simply a cloth tied around your waist with a flap in the back. You brought the flap up between your legs and tucked it under and over the piece around your waist in the front. Those were our under shorts. We decided to send in two men at a time. The height of the cloth went from the floor to just below your armpit. One guy would lift his arm up and back into the roll and turn around a few times until he was wrapped up, then we would cut it. The next guy would do the same until we all finished and hurried stiffly back to our detail. You see, when we marched as a group, we just kind of slouched and walked in somewhat of a formation to the Japanese cadence. But on this day, watch out West Point, we were stiff as boards and marched with precise turns and steps. We were marching as if it was pass and review time at West Point because the cloth was wrapped around us like a mummy wrap from the arm pits down. It was so funny we all started cracking up back at camp. What was even funnier was when we tried to make our shorts. Some of the guys could not sew or cut equal sides so some would be too tight and some would have one leg longer than the other. This was a great time in all the chaos that surrounded us. We were eventually transferred to another camp because this camp closed on May 20th, 1945.

Maibara Camp

On May 21st, 1945, we arrived at Maibara. This was the last camp where I would be stationed. It was next to Lake Biwa, one of the largest lakes in Japan. It was located at UMEGAHARA, SHIGA-ken, SAKATA-gun, MAIBARA-machi off National Route 8, which was south of the Maibara train station. The Camp Commander was Kohkichi Asakawa. The guards were Sergeant Fujiki Fumio and Superior Private Taguchi. The Civilian guards were Ito Eiichi, Takeda Fusatsugu, Rikiya Sane, and Genjiro Tuchkikawa.

The work we did here was reclaiming land from Lake Biwa so we could make farm fields out of it. We would have to go into the water, dam it up with dikes, and drain it to cultivate the soil. It was hard work but at least we got to get in the water and cool off. The downside was that our feet were always wet and muddy. Every once in a while, the detail guard would let us dive for these black clams that were in the lake. They are similar to oysters and tasted good when you're hungry. On the days we would do this, one or two prisoners would stay back and boil some lake water in a couple of pots. When we got out of the water with our clams, we would take them over to the pots, open them up, scoop everything out, I mean everything, throw it into the pots, and eat them right there. We did not let anything go to waste, ever. They only gave us about ten minutes to do that, so one day I was a little slow to get out of the water when it was time to get out. The guard yelled again to get out. Well I finally got out and got into the group but he did not know for sure who it was. He wanted to know who it was, but no one said anything. We have a code that when you are in a large group like that and you mess up, you step forward so the rest do not get punished. I finally stepped forward and he walked over to me and punched me right in the face. It hurt a lot, but the rest of the guys were glad I stepped forward so they didn't have to get punched as well.

After our hard day's work, we would walk back to camp along a road with houses on both sides. As always, we were looking for something to eat. Well there were always chickens running around on the same road also. You know how stupid chickens are. When we walked by them they got skittish and didn't know which way to run. Well the ones that would try to run across the road and cut through the formation never made it across. It's was kind of funny to hear the chicken cackling as it was running then all of a sudden there's silence. The POWs who were the closest would reach down, grab it by the neck, and shove it into their shirts with a little twist at the end. The poor bird ended up being plucked back at camp and given to the cook for our meal. We had to survive by any means we could by whatever means we could and we took what the good Lord gave us. He didn't give us a chicken everyday but he did on more than one occasion.

When we would get back to camp we would have other details and chores we would have to do. I would help Juan Paiz who was one of the fellow POW's I buddied with chop wood. During my free time, I would draw pictures or carve names for other POWs in exchange for food, or sometimes just for fun. There is a fellow POW who today lives in Victoria, Texas. His name is Raymond Villa and he was part of the 200th C.A. He was also another POW I buddied with. He still has a small wooden spoon that I carved his name in it for him. There is no telling how many mess kits, canteens, plates, spoons and pictures that I drew or carved over the years. I wish I could have some of those back—especially the flags.

One day, in the first week of August 1945, we woke up to go to work as usual. We grabbed our picks, shovels and whatever tools we needed for the days' work. The Japanese guards said that we did not have to go to work. We said, "What? No work?" We had been doing hard, dirty, painful, back-breaking, slave labor work for three and a half years, seven days a week, and now we don't have to go to work? We knew something was wrong because the guards would not tell us why. Well, we did not argue and just walked around camp and did our own thing. A few days later I was sitting outside in the yard of the camp. I was looking up at the clouds, because as an artist you tend to study their different shapes and colors. But on this day the clouds were very unusual. This particular cloud I was looking at was very tall and was rolling in and out of itself as if it was tumbling. It had a real pretty pinkish color with the blue sky background to it. I told the Japanese guard there, "Look how pretty that cloud is." He had a real sad face and just turned away without looking at it. It was the most beautiful cloud I had ever seen. A few more days had passed and still we had no work. We were beginning to wonder what was going on. Then one day, the train came by our camp and stopped right outside. Normally the train did not stop. It usually had Japanese soldiers and equipment on it. This day it did not. When it stopped, a soldier dressed in clean khakis got off the train and started to walk towards our camp. We could see this through the holes in the fence and from the tops of the roofs of our barracks. The POWs who were looking through would give us a play-by-play detail. "He's getting off the train. He's walking our way. He's coming to our gate." This was very unusual, because all we had seen for three and a half years were Japanese. He walked up to our main gate and yelled to open it up. The Japanese guards who were on duty did not move. They did not know what to do. We opened the gate and he said something I will never forget. He said, "What are you guys doing? Don't you know the war is over? Japan has surrendered." We said, "What, Japan has surrendered?" Boy you could've heard us hollering all the way to the United States. It was a joy you cannot understand. We thought to ourselves, "If the war is over, then why are there still guards here and why did they not tell us?" That beautiful cloud I had seen a few days earlier was the bomb that was dropped on Nagasaki. It had been dropped at 11:02 am on August 9th, 1945. We decided to test out the Japanese to see if that was true. They had stacked their rifles by the guard house where they were sitting so we started towards them. Some of us went for the rifles and some of us went for the guards. Just as soon as we grabbed the rifles, they got scared and tried to grab them, too. A tug of war ensued for the rifles until they gave up and ran off. I looked over towards my left and saw the Japanese camp interpreter who translated English to Japanese trying to sneak away. I grabbed two of my buddies and said "Let's go get him." All we were going to do was scare him. He didn't see us at first, but when he did, he started walking faster so we walked faster. Then he started to run, so we started to run faster. Before you know it, he was out the back gate by the kitchen running down the road. We picked up a few rocks and started throwing them at him not trying to hurt him, but to give him a good scare.

By August 15th, 1945, all the guards were gone and we had control of the camp. We tore down some of the fences and went about the countryside looking for food and whatever else we could get. A bunch of us went to the train station once in Maibara and boarded a train full of civilians and soldiers. We started taking the swords, knives and guns from the soldiers. They did not resist us. I kept one of the swords and went on my way back to camp. Some of the other guys went traveling, even going to other cities. I guess the American Government made the Japanese give out all the locations of the camps, because a few days later a Navy plane flew over and circled a few times. We had some Navy guys with us so they ran and got some sticks and tied white flags on the end and started signaling them. I don't know what they said to each other but the next day the pilot came back, made a few passes until he got into the right position, and then dropped a ham and a white duffle bag full of supplies that went right through the roof of the Camp Commander's quarters. The thing in that bag I remember the most was the coffee. If you had not smelled coffee for three and a half years, and all of a sudden here it was, you don't know what you're missing. Not long after that we got supplies dropped from B-29 bombers that flew overhead. They were fifty-five gallon drums attached to multi-colored parachutes full of clothes, first aid items, and more supplies. Since I was the camp artist, the Warrant Officer in charge, Frank Schratz, asked me to take the different colored parachutes and have some flags made. I had to draw the different flag designs for all the POWs who were there, including Americans, Australians, British, and Dutch. I drew the designs and took the material to a Japanese tailor who lived close by. I gave him three days to make the flags. On the third day I went to get the flags and paid him with some vegetables and supplies we had there at camp. You see the Japanese civilians were just as bad off as we were, so he was glad to get the food and supplies. I took the flags back, tied them to some bamboo poles and hung them up right outside the gate. As we started to raise the flags someone said "hey we need some instruments to play our national anthems." So some of the guys went back into town and found some so the National Anthem was played for each country as we raised each flag. It was one of the most beautiful sights I have ever seen. Freedom is something that is treasured by me very deeply. After suffering beatings, torture, and starvation for three and a half years, I cried and cried. It was so beautiful to see that American flag flying in the air. So many great men and women had died for those flags and the countries they represented. After the ceremony, we drew straws to see who would get the flags. They said to give the American flag to Ortega since he was the one who had them made. I said whoever gets the short straw can have it. I wish now that I had kept it. I don't know where the flags are today, but I just hope they are in a museum somewhere for all to see what the cost of freedom is and what they represent.

National Archives

Maibara Camp Photo taken Sept. 7th, 1945 from a plane off the USS Bon Homme Richard, CV31.

The small building on the lower left corner was the kitchen and the back gate where I chased the Japanese interpreter out of and down the road.

National Archives

Maibara Camp Photo taken Sept. 7th, 1945 from a plane off the USS Bon Homme Richard, CV31

There are the flags that I had made flying proudly at the entrance to the camp.

NAME. ORTEGA, ABEL F.	DATE OF ~~CAPTURE~~ BIRTH. Aug. 22, 1919
PLACE OF BIRTH. EL PASO, TEXAS	JAPANESE P.O.W. NO. 9972
	PLACE OF CAPTURE: BATAAN
DOMICILE 505 E. 9th St.	STATE OF HEALTH. FAIR
RANK PVT.	REMARKS.
NAME OF UNIT AT TIME OF CAPTURE: 192 TANK BN. CO. A	
	CAMP AND DATE X AUG. 27, 1945
ARMY NO 38029189	SIGNATURE: Abel F. Ortega

National Archives

POW card from Maibara.
My POW # is 9972

Photo # NH 97341 USS Bon Homme Richard off New York City, January 1945

Navy. History. Mil

USS Bon Homme Richard CV31

The following 3 pictures are from Camp Maibara after the war was over. They were taken on October 15th, 1945. This is the road back to the front gate. We walked up and down this road everyday back to Camp after a hard day's work.

This is the view coming in the front gate, walking past the guard house on the right. My barrack was the first one past the guard house on the right.

This is the back view of the bath house and the left rear corner of my Barrack.

These 3 photos are from Mr. Toru Fukubayashi

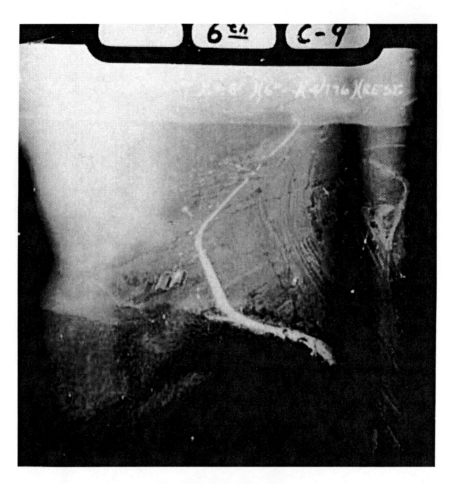

Camp Maibara

Mr. Toru Fukubayashi

This is the view from the back of one of the B-29 Bombers dropping our food and supplies in fifty-five gallon drums by parachutes. If you look closely, you can see some of the parachutes. It was these parachutes I used to make the flags at our camp.

We would walk out of the front of the camp, turn right and walk down to the main road you see in the picture. My detail would turn left and walk up the road to Lake Biwa where we did our reclamation of farm land from the lake.

The Trip Home

I left Maibara on **September** 9th, 1945, and headed for Yokohama, **Japan,** by train. The train arrived at Yokohama the next day, where I was deloused, bathed and given **more** clean clothes. Those of us on the docks boar**de**d the USS Benevolence AH13, which was hospital **ship** docked there at Yokohama. They let us eat whatever we wanted. We had eggs, bacon, toast and all the foods we had missed over the years. Since I was in pretty good health, I was able to leave a few days later.

Navy. History. Mil

USS Benevolence AH13

On September 12th, 1945, I boarded the USS Goodhue APA 107 and headed back to Manila to be shipped back to The United States. I arrived in Manila and was sent to the 29th Replacement Depot, where we lived in tents because there were so many of us arriving from different areas. I was only there for a week when I finally headed home to the good old U.S.A. I arrived in San Francisco on Oct. 15, 1945, and was taken to Letterman Hospital for another check-up and out-processing. I was finally able to call home and talk to my parents. There was only one problem. When I left for the Philippines I was only 21 years old. I was now 26 years old and my voice had changed. My dad did not believe it was me at first. He gave the phone to mama and she knew it was me when I started to ask for rice, frijoles, tortillas, enchiladas, and so on. I was so happy to hear their voices. It was through their prayers that I was able to survive what I had been through.

When I arrived back in Austin, Texas, I got off that Greyhound bus and the sword I carried fell out of the scabbard and went clanging down the steps onto the ground. There were people jumping to get out of the way because they had not seen one of those before and did not know what to expect. I just bent over, picked the sword back up, put it back into the scabbard and went on my way. I took a taxi home and when I pulled up to the steps, dad was waiting there for me. I went to give him a big hug but he would not take it. He wanted mama to get the first hug. He yelled, "menna," which is what he called her, "Your son Abelito is here!" I saw mama walking toward the door as she was wiping her hands on her apron. That was the most beautiful sight I had seen in my life. I cried and hugged my mama for a long, long time. It was my mother's prayers that kept me alive all those years. My sister said she could hear mama praying all night long for me to be safe and for God to bring me back home. I was truly blessed to have such a wonderful family that prayed for me. I was so glad to be back home.

Afterword

After the war was over I met a beautiful woman named Naomi Rodriguez from Dilley, Texas, who I made my wife on December 29th, 1946. We bought a house that was only available to Veterans after the war, located at 902 Jewel Street. The house still stands today.

December 29th, 1946

I had two children by 1950, when I was called back up to go fight in Korea. Needless to say, I did not want to go because I had seen enough war, death and destruction, but my duty called. I was there from November of 1950 to June of 1951. They assigned me to the 3rd Division, 15th Infantry Regiment.

We moved to San Antonio in 1957 and continued to raise our children. In 1966 our last child was born. We ended up being blessed by God with seven wonderful children. They are Deborah, Daniel, Ruth, Susanna, Priscilla, Abel, and Diane.

Abel Sr., Mom, Deborah, Daniel, Ruth, Susanna, Priscilla, Abel Jr., and Diane

All in all, I am proud of the 100 percent service I gave for my country. I wore that Army uniform proudly through two wars and have the utmost respect for the American flag and what it stands for. So many people have lost their lives for their country and I shall forever salute and remember those who never came back.

Abel F. Ortega, 2003   **Abel and Naomi Ortega, 2003**

In the end, Dad would receive The Bronze Star, three Purple Hearts, a Prisoner of War Medal, a Good Conduct Medal with two Awards, an American Defense Service Medal with a Foreign Clasp, an American Campaign Medal, an Asiatic-Pacific Campaign Medal with two Bronze Stars, a World War II Victory Medal, an Army of Occupation Medal with a Japan Clasp, a National Defense Service Medal, a Korean Service Medal with two Bronze Stars, Philippine Defense Medal with one Bronze Star, a Philippine Liberation Medal, a Philippine Independence Medal with one Bronze Star, a United Nations Service Medal, a Republic of Korean War Service Medal, an Army Presidential Unit Citation with two Oak Leafs, a Philippine Presidential Unit Citation, a Korean Presidential Unit Citation, a Combat Infantrymen Badge 1st Award with a Wreath, eight Overseas Bars, and two Service Stripes.

Throughout this book I have tried to tell about Dad's experiences through his words. This book covers just a small portion of what he actually went through. I am glad that Dad has shown the courage to talk with me about his experiences, because some POWs will not talk at all. Three and a half years worth of beatings, starvation and torture carry painful memories. I know it was a painful recollection for him at times, but he knows that these stories must be told. The men of WWII are dying by the hundreds everyday without their stories being told, and that is a tremendous loss for us. Those men on Bataan who were abandoned, forgotten, and surrendered to the Japanese showed extraordinary perseverance, courage, and a will to survive beyond their years. This is something that cannot be fully explained in this book or for any of us to try to understand. These men were part of the greatest generation to have lived. The sacrifices these men made on the battlefields for our freedom should not be forgotten.

The immeasurable strength and fortitude my dad showed, and the promise to God he made to help his fellow soldiers, even when he had chances to escape, tells what kind of man he is. Over the years, my family and I have always looked to him for strength and guidance when we needed it. I know his faith in God has helped keep him a strong man, both mentally and physically, even at 85. He has been a pillar of strength and wisdom for our family and always will.

To me, this man is the true meaning of what a Hero is. If I could be just a quarter of the man he is, it would be an honor. Thanks, Dad, for what you did for our country, and always remember that you are my hero. God has blessed me with the greatest father anyone could ever ask for. I love you, Dad, and I am honored to be your son!

Bibliography

1. www.mansell.com/pow-index.html Thanks to Roger Mansell for his wealth of knowledge about the POW Camps in the Far East, offering expert guidance and for use of the Bilibid Prison photo.
2. www.west-point.org/family/japanese-pow/ Thanks to the entire List serve members for their replies with answers and help to my many questions.
3. "Death on Hellships" by Greggory Michno, published by Naval Institute Press. He has done the most accurate research about the Hell Ships, and their voyages. Thanks for the use of his convoy numbers and Hell Ship casualty information.
4. www.proviso.k12.il.us/Bataan%20Web/index.htm Proviso East High School Commemorative Research Project. Thanks to Jim Opolony for his undying effort to honor all the men of the 192nd Tank Battalion Companies and for the use of some Death March photos.

5. "Japanese Merchant Ships at War" by Hisashi Noma. Thanks to him for the use of the Melbourne Maru Picture and ship information.
6. "3.6 Years of Hell" by Joe Lajzer, published by The Watercress Press. He is a wonderful and trusted friend of my father who was in Company B of the 192nd Tank Battalion and most of the same camps.
7. Thanks to Nori Nagasawa who lives in Yokohama, Japan. She traveled many miles in Japan in search of the POW Camps, locations and the men who were there both American and Japanese. Her research is invaluable and appreciated.
8. Thanks to the U.S. National Archives in Baltimore, Maryland where I obtained photographs and documents pertaining to the POWs of WWII in the Philippines, Formosa and Japan.
9. www.powtaiwan.org Thanks to Michael Hurst for his dedication to the POW Camps in Formosa, now Taiwan, the POWs that were there, their locations, and the use of the map of Formosa and The Camp Toroku drawing.
10. Thanks to www.harrisonheritage.com and all the members who have put together a wonderful web site dedicated to the American Defenders of Bataan and Corregidor and for the use of the Hell Ship document.
11. Thanks to http://www.history.navy.mil for the photos of the USS Benevolence and USS Bon Homme Richard
12. Thanks to www.sfps.k12.nm.us/academy/bataan/main.html which is a collaborative project and web site dedicated to the Bataan Death

140

March and for their use of the Death March Route map.

13. Thanks to Thore Kibsgaard for the photo of the Hokusen Maru. His father, Torvald A. Kibsgaard, was on the same "Hell Ship" as my father.

14. Thanks to Duane Heisinger of www.fatherfound. com for the forward, and for his guidance and support throughout this project. His book *Father Found* published by Xulon Press, is a book of love and respect for his Father who, too, was a POW along with my father.

15. Thanks to Mr. Toru Fukubayashi, author of *The Last Missions of the B-29 Bombers*, for the photo of the food drops over Camp Maibara and the post-war photos of the camp.

Printed in the United States
137028LV00004B/6/A